TOP SECRETS
LESSONS FOR SUCCESS FROM THE WORLD OF ESPIONAGE

Keith Massey, PhD

Lingua Sacra Publishing

Top Secrets: Lessons for Success from the World of Espionage
Copyright © 2015 by Keith Massey

All rights reserved.
Published in the United States by
Lingua Sacra Publishing.
www.linguasacrapublishing.com
ISBN 978-0-9843432-7-0

Dedication

To David and Jennifer.

About the Author

Keith Massey, PhD, is the author of *Intermediate Arabic for Dummies,* a number of fiction novels, and numerous academic articles on biblical, linguistic, and historical topics. He worked as an Arabic linguist for the National Security Agency. He is currently a language instructor.

Legal Disclaimer

The views and opinions expressed in this work are the author's and not that of the National Security Agency or the US Government.

Also By Keith Massey

Fiction

A Place of Brightness

Amor Vincit Omnia: An Andrew Valquist Adventure

Next Stop: Spanish

In Saecula Saeculorum

Non-Fiction

Intermediate Arabic for Dummies

Praying Our Fathers: The Secret Mercies of Ancestral Intercession

Top Secrets: Lessons for Success from the World of Espionage

Introduction 1

Part One: My Life As A Spy

Chapter One: My Journey To The NSA 7
Chapter Two: Inside The NSA (2002-2004) 27
Chapter Three: Inside The NSA (2004-2006) 81
Chapter Four: How I Got My Medal 97

Part Two: Using Lessons from Intelligence Analysis For Personal and Professional Success

Chapter Five: HUMINT
(Human Intelligence) 105
Chapter Six: SIGINT
(Signals Intelligence) 117
Chapter Seven: OPSEC
(Operations Security) 127
Chapter Eight:
Deciphering Secret Codes 135
Chapter Nine: Living Your Cover 157
Chapter Ten: Resources For Learning More 165

Appendix

The Three Month Productivity Plan of the Ancients 171

Introduction

Rationale For This Book

We are each juggling so many personal and professional responsibilities that we are always interested in any information or inspiration that might give us an edge. As a result, books on productivity and motivation enjoy perennial popularity.

The fact is, we already know deep down what we have to do to be successful. Hard work and perseverance, coupled with a bit of luck from time to time, is a tried and true winning formula. But we are challenged to excellence by hearing the testimony of others who achieved success in their goals. And we can take a new and creative perspective to our own situation when we view the steps to success through some new lens or paradigm.

Even so, we also know from personal experience that there are those succeed in both their professional and personal dealings without playing fair. There are those who sabotage, cheat and steal both in terms of material goods but also in the realm of ideas.

And that is why it struck me that a knowledge of how nations and other transnational entities (such as , for instance, terrorist organizations) perform these "activities" within the realm of espionage could be a particularly valuable asset to people in both business and personal matters.

I served as an Arabic Linguist at the National Security Agency for four years after 9/11. Experiences I had at the NSA continue to inform how I approach elements of my personal and professional life.

But also, on a practical level, a knowledge of the disciplines, means, and methods of espionage equip a person in the corporate world with the tools necessary to combat (and, I suppose, to perform) espionage both between competing entities and in the cutthroat world within one's own office. Indeed, the means and methods are largely identical.

I was, frankly, surprised to find that little literature in this vein already existed. And so, I have addressed the gap with this current book.

Few people experience the world of espionage from the inside. And, as I'll explain, those of us who have worked on the inside are restricted from divulging certain details of what we know even after we leave. But I've carefully recounted my story in a way that allowed what I publish here to be approved by government censors.

Format Of This Book

This book is not designed to be read necessarily from start to finish. A reader could begin, for instance, with topics in Part Two of particular importance and interest to them first.

In Part One, I tell the story of how I came to be a Top Secret agent at the National Security Agency. But this story is not a straightforward biography. I share with you the life lessons I learned on my way into the world of espionage, and my adventures and struggles during my time on the inside. I detail areas where I met with failure, as well as success. I am very proud of the career I describe in Part One, and if my experiences inspire anyone to persevere in their own context, I will be happy to have helped them even in some small measure.

Part Two describes several specific disciplines within the world of espionage and how a knowledge of various issues in the spy world can help you in your personal and professional contexts.

Finally, I also include as an appendix the description of an ancient productivity plan I discovered while serving in Iraq in 2004.

Strengths and Applications of the Espionage Paradigm

Like our personal and professional lives, the world of Intelligence gathering and analysis (AKA espionage) is multi-faceted. Undercover spies buying secrets in a back alley face different challenges than spies listening in on a phone call. Analysts then use a diverse set of intelligence data to draw conclusions to help policy makers decide on their best course of action. Doesn't that sound just like the decision making process inside any business entity? (I mean, hopefully, without the back alley dealings, etc.)

But what makes the science of intelligence analysis a particularly profitable paradigm through which to draw motivation and lessons on productivity is the fact that intelligence analysis has sometimes and famously failed! And when it fails, the ramifications can be disastrous and even deadly. When something goes wrong, when an intelligence report fails to provide appropriate information, government officials understandably want to know how and why the failure occurred. If it happened through negligence, the responsible party must face consequences. (And in this book I'll tell you the story of a time I screwed up significantly.) Most importantly, if an intelligence report fails to provide accurate and necessary information, government officials want to make sure that such mistakes are not repeated.

As a result, by my experience, the field of intelligence gathering and analysis is constantly introspective on its own methods, in order to perform its role with ever greater effectiveness. A knowledge, then, of the best practices of Intelligence analysis can benefit a wide range of sectors, from the business world to private individuals seeking to achieve their own definition of success.

PART ONE: MY LIFE AS A SPY

CHAPTER ONE: MY JOURNEY TO THE NSA

Like so many people, I sat watching the news on September 11, 2001 in pure shock. I gave blood the next day, like thousands of concerned citizens around the country who simply wanted to do something, anything, in response to this senseless tragedy.

I also saw that the major television news outlets were running a ticker at the bottom of the screen, telling anyone with expertise in Arabic language to consider sending their resumes to the intelligence agencies. I just happened to have expertise in that area. I had my PhD in Biblical Hebrew with a minor in Arabic from the University of Wisconsin-Madison.

And so, out of duty and patriotism, I sent my resume online to the National Security Agency and the Central Intelligence Agency. It was the least I could do. I mean, after all, we had been attacked and we also expected a follow-on attack imminently.

The Back Story

My parents had come from the rural town of Barneveld, Wisconsin, thirty miles west of Madison, the capital. How did the son of farmer stock end up with experience needed by the US in a war against terrorism?

First off, my twin brother Kevin and I had taken four years of Latin in high school, but I was personally quite worthless in languages at that time. My teacher early on told me that, as long as I was not disruptive, I would get a C no matter what I did in the class. That can't have been legal, even in the early eighties!

Top Secrets

After we graduated from high school, we learned, just before registering for classes at the University of Wisconsin, that we could get sixteen credits from our high school work if we got a B or better in the fifth semester class of Latin. My twin brother and I both went for this prize. But I had one problem. Despite four years of enrollment in a high school Latin program, I really did not know anything of the language. I took personal responsibility for my ignorance and I checked out some books from the public library and began studying.

As the Latin class at the University actually started, I was discovering that I had a mind for languages, a thing I previously didn't know because of my own laziness and lack of applying myself in high school. My twin and I both worked very hard and achieved our goal. I got an A in the course and was offered a scholarship if I declared a Classics Major (Latin and Classical Greek). No brainer there. Follow the money.

I spent the next four years studying those classical languages in depth. I also picked up three semesters of Biblical Hebrew before graduating with my BA. I went to a seminary in Minnesota and got a Masters in Old Testament. And then I was offered a scholarship for the graduate studies program in Biblical Hebrew back at the University of Wisconsin. No brainer there. Keep following the money. And, as I told you, I eventually obtained my doctorate in Biblical Hebrew, with a minor in Arabic from that school.

So that explains how I had the expertise that qualified me to apply for a position at the National Security Agency as an Arabic linguist after 9/11. And it also explains why, when I eventually decided I had had enough espionage adventures, I could become a Latin teacher at a public high school, which is what I am today.

Getting Started

September 11, 2001 was a Tuesday. I sent my resume online to the NSA that Thursday the 13th. On Sunday, I received a reply. I got an email from the NSA asking me to call a number within 72 hours for an initial interview.

Top Secrets

Now, I'll be honest. By that point, I was a bit excited about the possibility of working for the NSA in our nation's time of crisis. And I assumed that this initial interview would involve some test of the language abilities I had claimed in my resume.

I left nothing to chance. I didn't call immediately, because I wanted to brush up on my Arabic skills and be the best I could possibly be for the test I assumed I was about to face.

And so, after 48 hours of non-stop study, I called the number I had been sent. I was ready for anything.

"Hello?"
"Yes, um, I was sent an email to call this number for an initial interview."
"Your Social Security Number, please?"
I provided it.
"You're Keith Massey?"
"Yes."

I braced myself. The language test was surely about to begin.

"I just have a few questions for you. First, are you a US Citizen?"

"Yes."

"Okay, good. Secondly, have you ever sold illegal drugs?"

"Um, no. Never."

"Good. We'll be getting in touch with you to arrange for your formal language testing here at the NSA as soon as possible."

And that was it! Here I was assuming they would test my language abilities over the phone, but all they were really doing in that first call was weeding out unacceptable candidates. Notice, they didn't ask me if I had ever *used* illegal drugs. Youthful indiscretions do not necessarily disqualify one from a Top Secret clearance. But trafficking in the stuff, well, that invalidates one forever.

They sent me an email with all the information I needed to make arrangements to travel to the NSA for my language testing. I seemed to be dealing ostensibly with a travel agency, but I imagined that the enterprise was probably something devoted solely to NSA recruitment activities. Over the phone with this travel agency, someone proposed potential dates of travel, less than a month in the future. I was informed that a shuttle at the airport would then take me to a hotel not far from an NSA facility called the Friendship Annex (FANX), where my testing would take place.

Still leaving nothing to chance, I studied hours on end in the couple of weeks I had before my formal testing. I particularly spent considerable time working on my listening and comprehension skills, which, because I am not a native speaker, had always been the weakest part of my language abilities.

First Visit to the NSA

Flying in the month immediately after 9/11 was somewhat surreal. There were armed National Guard soldiers all over Dane County Regional Airport in Madison, something I had never seen there before. Recall that prior to 9/11 there was no TSA. Each airport ran its own provincial security operation with little consistency or even rigor. I used to have a large jackknife attached to my keys. And every time I flew before 9/11, I would put that thing with my keys in a little bowl to pass around the x-ray machine before I went through. You see, they were only trying to screen for guns and bombs. And I can remember wondering why in the world it was okay for me to be bringing a large blade onto the plane. It took a disaster to make America realize that we shouldn't have allowed such things on planes after all.

As we were taxiing to the runway for my first flight, from Madison to Chicago, a man went berserk and was screaming that he needed to get off the plane. We taxied back and he was removed. This, of course, prompted all the other passengers to become concerned that the man in question might know something the rest of us didn't. We were told that the man would be detained at the airport until we had safely arrived in Chicago.

From Chicago it was direct to Baltimore/Washington International Airport. After getting settled into my hotel room, I did some last minute language study in preparation for the next day.

The tests were two-fold. First, I translated a written passage. I had access to a dictionary, which both surprised and relieved me. Then there was a listening passage to translate. I'll admit that I was additionally surprised that at the Top Secret and technologically advanced National Security Agency, this portion of the test used cassette players and tapes. I was physically hitting rewind on a machine to roll tape back to re-listen to the passage!

When it was all over, I felt very good about the text translation and not so good about the listening portion. There had been several spots in the recording where, despite listening to it over and over again, I couldn't make out anything that seemed to make sense. And with time running out, I ended up putting down something I knew wasn't completely correct, but that was better than leaving a hole in my translation.

The Results Come In

About a week after my testing, I got an email from the NSA. The message informed me that I had passed the graphic part of their exam (reading and translating), but that I had *not* passed the listening portion. And for that reason they would not pursue my potential employment any further.

I'm going to admit that I was deeply disappointed by this news. I had come to really anticipate serving my country at the NSA. It had been a few years since I finished my PhD and I had tried to keep up my Arabic skills, but I guess it wasn't enough.

Then everything suddenly changed again. A few days after the bad news, I got a call back that they were creating a program for certain select people that had passed only one of the required skills. They would hire us and then strengthen the deficient skill once we started work at the NSA. On the basis of my advanced degrees and other scholarship, I had been selected for this program. And so, they sent me all the documents I needed to fill out for the security background check.

What a rollercoaster of emotions the whole experience had been up to that point! I mean, first off, this was all happening in the days following 9/11, with the fear of follow-on attacks, and then the Anthrax Scare. What I've described thus far was also happening against the backdrop of preparations for and execution of the US invasion of Afghanistan. I had experienced the stress of immediately post-9/11 air travel. There was the excitement of the whole application and testing process. Then there was the crushing disappointment of failure. And now there was the sudden elation that this adventure was back on track.

I learned that the documents I needed to return would be used to conduct a Single Scope Background Investigation (SSBI), but that I would also be flown back to the NSA for a Full Scope/Lifestyle Polygraph test. This was all necessary to be approved for a Top Secret/Sensitive Compartmented Information clearance (TS/SCI), which all employees at the NSA are required to have.

On these forms, I had to provide the names and contact information for three people corresponding to everywhere I had lived, worked, or gone to school for the previous ten years. And no one could be listed in more than one category. And I needed to account for everywhere I had been, with no gaps whatsoever, for that time period.

About a month after I sent it all in, I got a call from the Department of Defense investigator in charge of my background check. He told me he needed to meet with me before he would then be traveling around the Madison area interviewing all the contacts I had provided. We met in an office at the main branch of the Madison Post Office. Apparently a DOD investigator can just call up a post office and say, "I need an office for a week. Make it so."

In my meeting with him, he primarily needed to clear up the fact that I had inadvertently left a gap of a week a few years back on my forms. It was a pure error, but he made me emend my supplied information.

Over the next several days I would get calls from people telling me that they had received a visit from the man, and that he had additionally asked them for names and contact information of people not supplied by me for the investigation.

Second Visit to the NSA

In January I was flown back for my polygraph test. I was once again at the FANX. I'll admit, I was very nervous, since I had never experienced such a thing before. My polygrapher wrapped this stuff like coiled telephone wire around my chest to measure my respiration. There was a little cuff on my finger to test perspiration. A blood pressure cuff was put on me as well.

And he proceeded to ask me questions such as "Are you now or have you ever been a member of an organization plotting the overthrow of the United States Government?"

"Nope, I am not."

I answered everything truthfully, but at one point the guy tells me that the test indicated that I was evasive on questions regarding whether I had ever sold illegal drugs. We even had a little showdown in which he said he would wait as long as it took for me to just admit that I had once sold illegal drugs. And I wasn't going to, since it simply wasn't true.

He eventually unhooked me and I assumed my chances of working at the NSA were finished. Just as I left the room, however, a man stopped me and told me that failing an initial polygraph is not uncommon and he would rebook my flights so I could try again the next day.

For that first polygraph test, I had dressed in slacks, a shirt, and a tie. The second time, I went wearing a t-shirt and sweat pants. I knew I just needed to relax. I had a different polygrapher, which is standard practice. In fact, he didn't redo the whole test. All he asked me was the specific question the previous polygrapher said I failed on. And this time I passed.

I was informed in the middle of February that I had my Top Secret clearance, but that they would not be equipped to bring in new employees until the middle of June. I was in one of the very first new "classes" of NSA agents after 9/11. I was sworn in on Monday, June 17, 2002.

And I could not possibly have imagined then, as I raised my right hand and took an oath to defend the Constitution of the United States, that just two years later, on June 17, 2004, I would be in US-occupied Iraq. But we'll get to that in chapter 2.

The Pre-Publication Review Process

Now, everything I've told you so far involved my processing prior to being officially under a Top Secret clearance and working inside the NSA. People that tried and failed to work there could have experienced, seen, and published reports of everything I've said so far. What I can say about the inside will be trickier.

The day I went to work at the NSA, I signed a document to the effect that I would submit everything I would ever publish in the future to pre-publication review, lest I even inadvertently reveal anything classified. And this book itself was thus submitted. They determined, despite my earnest efforts to avoid including anything classified in this manuscript, that there were two sentences I had to delete prior to publication. I don't necessarily have to agree with their position that the material was classified, but I did, of course, comply.

So the account I will make about my time inside the NSA was crafted to avoid anything truly Secret. For the purposes of this book, I'll focus primarily on what I learned and the lessons you may be able to take from it for your own professional or personal enrichment.

Life Lessons on the Way to the NSA

In chapters 2 and 3, I will describe my time as a spy at the NSA. But before I tell that story, I would like to share some thoughts about what I learned before then, in the process of applying for and successfully entering that Top Secret world.

I had studied Arabic very intensely while working on my PhD. But from the time I was last formally in an Arabic class until the moment I sat down for the NSA tests was a period of eight years. If I had done nothing with my Arabic in the intervening time, I would not have succeeded. But I had regularly reviewed everything I learned and even managed to expand my vocabulary base.

Even so, as I described, it still nearly wasn't enough! If they had not decided to admit people passing only one of the linguistic skills, well, I guess I wouldn't be writing this book!

A part of me thinks that subconsciously I knew the day would come when Arabic would change my life. There would be a few months in which I would kind of let things slide. And then, as if in a panic, I would head back into my studies. Perhaps God was whispering in my ear that I needed to stay sharp for the momentous time to come. But after the fact, I knew that nothing truly valuable comes easily. I had kept my language skills strong through long hours of hard work. Whatever you want in life, you must be prepared to work hard for it and earn it.

I also certainly had to learn how to cope with disappointment. I had initially applied out of duty, but I soon wanted very badly to succeed in the application process. And I would spend a couple of days needing to come to terms with my failure to achieve that goal, before I then learned I was being given a second chance.

A final lesson I had to learn in the process of applying for government service was patience. Like so many Americans after 9/11, I wanted in the fight. I wanted to do my part. And it would turn out that I happened to have skills of crucial importance to that cause. But the reality is that the world sometimes just moves very slowly. The NSA got by in the early days after 9/11 by calling a bunch of retired people back into service part time. And they did indeed mobilize immediately to ramp up for a major effort. But the sheer logistics of it—where would these new employees have their desks, how to buy and install all the infrastructure these people would work with—these things took time. Indeed, these things took months.

When I finally came in the door, some of those returned retirees were still around. And the fact is, I learned many important lessons about the mission of being an Arabic linguist at the NSA from them before they were phased out as the new hires were coming in. So it all worked out for the best.

Professional and Personal Applications

As I will describe in more detail in the next chapter, the program of hiring people such as myself, deficient in one skill but presumably trainable in that weakness, was very successful. And it implies that hiring managers with long-term thinking should be open minded about candidates who may not have specific experience in all the areas of intended employment. It's an example of the concept frequently described as "Hire the Person, Not the Skills." If a candidate exhibits abundant qualities that point to an industrious and effective employee, it's probably okay if some of the "required experience" is weak or even lacking.

It was only in retrospect that I could see how numerous decisions made my eventual employment at the NSA possible—the decision to chase the retroactive credits in Latin, following the money and acquiring the advanced degrees, regularly studying to keep my skills as sharp as possible. The implication is that the successful attainment of a lofty goal, be it personal, professional, or corporate, could be premised on a lengthy period of time and constructed from numerous intermediate steps.

Chapter Two: Inside the NSA (2002-2004)

My First Assignment: Get Up To Speed

I described in chapter 1 how I had been hired at the NSA despite the fact that I didn't pass the listening portion of the language tests. After a few days of new employee orientation (you know, the typical sessions where you learn about your health coverage, etc.), I was informed that I was being sent to a month long class, which would meet back at the FANX where I had taken the initial language exams and my infamous polygraph test.

This class would be an intensive lesson in listening and transcribing skills (the very thing I was weakest at). The entire course was unclassified. I have all of the tapes and texts from that course with me still today, and I use them regularly to keep my Arabic language skills sharp.

For eight hours every day, for an entire month, about ten of us, people just like me, new hires who had not passed the listening portion of the NSA Arabic test, were in a classroom as our primary assignment. We would listen to passages in Arabic and attempt to transcribe what we were hearing. Each passage was about two minutes long. They were an assortment of Voice of America news in Arabic, BBC, etc. This was given to us merely because it was a good representation of the level of language we might operationally need to process.

Day after day, we toiled at this. After we had attempted our transcription of the passages, our instructors went over them with us closely. The instructors gave us hints on how to hear subtle differences in sounds and do better the next time.

After a month, we were all transcribing these recordings better and faster than we ever imagined we could. Now, that's not really surprising. I had tried to hone my listening skills prior to my tests to join the NSA because I knew that was my weakest point. But I had never before had the luxury of spending eight hours a day on the task for an entire month. Let alone getting paid for it!

Our class had a final exam. We were all going to go and sit down once again and take the listening portion of the NSA Arabic test—in the very same room at the FANX where we had all failed that test a few months earlier.

Now, any time you take a test, you're nervous. But this was especially stressful. I mean, what if after all this I still didn't pass this test? I didn't even know what the implications were. Would they fire me after just one month of employment if I don't pass now?

I certainly felt better about my chances. I had worked hard. And you need to know, I had not just let this course alone be my preparation for this retake. I went home every day that month and studied vocabulary and listened to Arabic deep into the night. I was leaving nothing to chance.

When the results came in, we had all passed (80% was passing). I passed with a 96%. I'm pretty proud of that, given the fact that I had failed that test just nine months earlier.

Lessons Learned

The fact is, the NSA did a very smart thing in those early days after 9/11. They were willing to cultivate people who maybe didn't make the initial cut but still showed promise. People like me. And it paid off for them.

Isn't that, in and of itself, an important lesson for our lives? I'm reminded of a quote:

> I have long been disposed to judge men by their average. If it is reasonably high, I am charitable with faults that look pretty black.
> Ed Howe

The NSA took a chance on me. I mean, what if they had hired me and then I never did develop the ability to perform listening skills operationally? And the takeaway is that, in both our personal and professional lives, it pays off to have a certain tolerance of others' weaknesses. Giving people the chance to improve, even after they have failed, can be a wise investment in potential resources for the future.

But another lesson I learned for myself is that one really can hone a skill by intense and intentional practice. Here I am reminded of a Latin quote:

assiduus usus, uni rei deditus, et ingenium et artem, saepe vincit.
Constant practice, given to one thing, often beats both genius and talent.[1]

My linguistic strengths still primarily reside in grammar and translation. I just don't have a natural talent for listening and comprehending a foreign language. But I was able to make up for that deficit by applying myself specifically in the area of my weakness.

So whatever skill you believe would advance your personal and professional life, get to work! Work on it even a little bit each day. Take personal responsibility that it is up to you to sharpen your skills and become the person who will succeed.

---

[1] Cicero, *Pro Balbo* 45.

My Second Assignment: Settling in at the NSA

After I had passed the listening portion of the NSA tests, I was assigned to an office where I would work for only a few months. But they were good months, in which I became acclimated to the NSA and began discovering how the operation worked.

I learned early on that we linguists were expected to be attempting our way through a series of tests called the Professional Qualification Exams (PQE).[2] There were four in all and they were offered every six months. There was an unclassified graphic translation (that is, some written text you translated). There was also a similar test, but translating something obtained in classified sources. You were not allowed to take the classified version until after you passed the unclassified one.

On the listening side, there was an unclassified test in which you transcribed an Arabic audio

---

[2] Since I've left the NSA, the PQE system has been completely replaced by a different language testing regime.

recording (that is, you wrote down exactly what you thought you heard). And, understandably, the final test was a classified version of the listening exam.

I learned that people who had never passed even one of the PQE's were still functioning as full time linguists at the NSA. So why bother taking these tests at all? For starters, you could not be assigned to an overseas assignment if you had not passed at least one of the PQE's. If you wanted the possibility of the adventure (and financial benefits) of such a deployment, you needed to pass those tests.

You also could not be appointed to the role of a Quality Controller unless you had passed them. Quality Control (QC) is the practice of always having a senior linguist confirm the accuracy of a translation before a report could be issued based on that work.

Finally, if you passed all four of the PQE's, you were then called "Professionalized." And this meant that you would receive "Foreign Language Incentive Pay" (FLIP). And it was substantial. Now, these tests were considerably more difficult than the ones to merely qualify for employment at the NSA. Indeed, these tests should be difficult, if so much is at stake.

Time For More Tests

I signed up to take the first PQE I could. Now, keep in mind, I was already functioning as an Arabic linguist at the NSA. I don't want to give you the impression that all I did was to take tests. Within my regular workload, I informed my boss that I was taking my first PQE. You were allotted two hours off from work to take the test, but otherwise you spent the rest of the day doing those things that Arabic linguists at the NSA do.

That first PQE was the unclassified graphic test. I left there feeling pretty good. I believed I might have passed the thing. But when I got the results, I had not only *not* passed, I was not even close!

I learned that if you do badly enough on a PQE, you are disqualified from taking that particular test six months later (out of the reasonable assumption that no one is really going to work a miracle in only six months and therefore the senior linguists who score these tests could reduce unnecessary workload). I had not done *that* badly on my first PQE attempt, but it was a wake-up call.

Just a few days later, I attempted the unclassified listening PQE. I left that one knowing I had certainly *not* passed. And then I got the news I was fearing. I failed so badly that I was disqualified from the listening test in the next round! I would not be allowed to take the unclassified listening test again for an entire year.

Now, based on what I've already told you, it's not surprising that I would bomb the listening PQE. I had not initially passed the listening test to even get hired at the NSA. Yes, I had later passed it after a month of intense practice, but the PQE's were a quantum leap beyond those pre-employment tests.

I was a little demoralized. But I vented that energy into a continued commitment to spend even a little time each evening at home practicing my listening skills. I was working beside some people who had been at the NSA for ten or more years and had never passed so much as *one* PQE, and had even stopped trying. The tests were that hard. That relieved me a little bit. But I didn't stop my efforts.

My Next Assignment: Learn a New Dialect

As the Fall of 2002 began, the big news in the world was the potential of a US invasion of Iraq to unseat Saddam Hussein. In anticipation of this possibility, the NSA understandably took measures to bolster its ability to process Intelligence in the Iraqi specific dialect of Arabic. I was offered the chance to attend an intensive Iraqi Dialect training class at NSA Georgia, which is located at Fort Gordon in Augusta, GA. For five weeks my full time job there was to study and prepare myself to be using the Iraqi dialect in an operational context once I returned to the main NSA campus at Fort Meade, MD.

My flight to Georgia included the only time I have ever been part of an emergency landing. I was sitting near the rear of the plane. I, and many other people there, began to smell the unmistakable odor of something burning. We didn't see smoke, but the smell was strong and worrisome. A flight attendant concurred and the plane made an unplanned landing in North Carolina. After a few hours, we were all rebooked on a different plane and resumed our journey.

I made the most of my training in Georgia. After eight hours of solid study during the day, I continued studying into the night. Remember, I still had those PQE's in my sights.

Yet Another Office

Upon my return to Fort Meade, I was immediately reassigned to an office focused on an aspect of Intelligence in Iraq. As the apparently inevitable war crept closer, our office divided into shifts so that we could provide 24/7 coverage for the military and policy makers. I volunteered for the third shift, 10:30PM to 7:00AM and, because I was distinguishing myself linguistically, I was appointed the team leader over my shift.

You might be surprised to learn that, even though I was a Top Secret cleared Arabic linguist at the National Security Agency working in an office related to Iraq, I had no idea when the war was actually going to start. I was at home getting ready to go in for my shift when I saw the "Shock and Awe" attack begin.

The overnight shift in the US is essentially the morning to mid-afternoon in Iraq, so my live-time support of the war effort was an exciting experience.

Passing PQE's

No sooner was the ground war over, that I was sent back to my original office, where I had not worked for seven months since the Iraq War preparations had begun. In the Summer that followed, I passed my first PQE, the unclassified graphic test. But I was still disqualified from attempting the unclassified listening test for another six months.

I continued to work hard and take classes offered at the NSA to make an employee operationally more proficient. So, for instance, I had the opportunity to take a week-long course in cryptographic methods. It basically covered everything on the subject up until the time when rudimentary computers took over during WWII.

In the next PQE cycle, I passed the classified graphic test with honors, for which they gave me a little trophy I still have in my office. And then I passed the unclassified listening PQE! Just a year earlier I had failed that test miserably. But a year of further work and study had made the difference.

And so, a year after I first attempted a PQE, I had passed three of the four. In other words, all I needed to get that FLIP pay was to pass one more test, the classified listening PQE. And I would certainly be attempting it in the next testing cycle.

Little did I know the circumstances under which I would end up attempting that final test just six months later.

Lessons Learned

The life lesson I learned in passing that unclassified listening PQE was the sheer power of perseverance. Failing the test and being disqualified was horribly discouraging. I could have just quit trying. But I didn't. I kept constantly working toward my goal.

I will say this. If there is a skill you know will set you apart, you can't just use work hours to hone it. You need to own your deficits and work until you make up for them, even if that means working on these things on your own time. That's what I had done throughout my first year at the NSA.

First Deployment

In the Spring of 2004, my boss came to me and offered me an opportunity. It was certainly something I could turn down if I was not interested. I was offered the chance to do a three month deployment in Iraq.

Keep in mind, in 2004 we were still the occupying force in that country. All US personnel, whether they were military or civilian, whether they were in the State Department or, well, something else, were required to carry a sidearm. And to do that, you had to be officially certified on the ability to safely and accurately fire the weapons you would need to carry.

Learning to Fire a Gun

Here's the story of how I got qualified to carry a sidearm and then went to Iraq. The NSA has its own weapons certification center, as you'd expect. But I totally lucked out and managed to get a slot at something infinitely sexier. I got to spend a week being certified on the Glock 9mm Handgun and the M-4 Assault Rifle at a secret CIA training facility somewhere in [Name of Area Withheld by Censor]. In fact, when my boss got me that slot, she asked me not to talk about it openly because the other NSA'ers would be jealous of the opportunity I had.

What made it so envious? Well, at the NSA facility, you just got basic certification. You were taught how to fire the gun and after you completed a test of firing a full clip on a target, you got your certification and you were good to go into the field.

Not so at the CIA. We didn't just fire the guns to achieve quick certification. It was a five day program that turned into quite the adventure.

We started the first day at a large shed of sorts, in which we had initial briefings on the week of training to come. There were somewhere between ten and fifteen of us in that group of trainees. That very first day, the trainers announced to the group that one of us was, gasp, an NSA'er. (Among the various intelligence agencies, there is a stereotype that NSA'ers are just a bunch of technical and linguistic nerds.) I laughed along with the rest as they joked that we would all know who he was when we first fired the guns and someone hit the ground trying to hide. Very funny guys. Let's just see if you can really spot me.

The very able trainers began to explain that they would be meticulously teaching us every aspect of these guns and how to fire them. Still in the shed, we learned for a couple of hours how to take the weapons apart and reassemble them.

I began to suspect that I had a secret advantage. You see, I had never before fired a handgun. And that meant I had no bad habits to unlearn either.

Top Secrets

I was *Tabula Rasa*, which, snickering CIA guys, is Latin for "Blank Slate." And you can draw anything on a Blank Slate, such as a good shot on those guns.

This all became apparent that first day when we finally went out to the range with our handguns. And our trainers told us to do EXACTLY as we were told.

Got it, trainers. I'll do exactly as I'm told. We don't have any bullets in our guns yet, by the way.

"Take your gun out of your holster and aim it down range."

I do as I'm told. I take my gun from its holster and I aim it down range.

We all hear several clicks up and down the range. The lead trainer walks slowly to the front of the group.

"WHO TOLD YOU TO PULL THAT TRIGGER?!" he screamed.

I had not pulled *my* trigger. After all, I had only been told to take the gun from the holster and point it down range. I know how to follow directions.

He screamed at us for several more minutes and told us that we were all now to put our guns back in the holster and we were going to repeat this exercise. And further he told us that anyone who ever pulled their trigger again, without being told to do so, would be sent home without the certification.

Once more, on orders, we pulled our guns from the holsters and pointed them down range. Now no one pulled the trigger.

We repeated that exercise several more times. Then came the order to pull the guns from the holster and this time pull the trigger.

We comply. And we do that several more times. Remember, we don't have bullets in our guns yet. We're just practicing the moves. The trainers keep telling us that we are repeating these moves so laboriously because we are building muscle memory. We will never practice firing that gun without first pulling it from the holster because, in the field, that's exactly what would happen.

It was late in that first morning. My stomach was growling. We knew a box lunch was waiting for us back at the shed. We were all issued ear plugs and shooting-range ear muffs and told to put on that gear.

"Release your clips!" the lead trainer shouted.

He then walked the length of the line and handed each of us a single cartridge.

"Load that into your clip and insert it."

I did as I was told.

"Pull back on the gun to chamber that shot."

I did as I was told.

"Put your guns back in their holsters."

We waited in silence for our next command.

"When I give the order, you will draw your guns from their holsters and then line up the target with the sight at the end of the barrel. Remember. This is not a race. When you have the sight on the target, take a breath and then release it and pull the trigger."

We stood looking down range at the paper targets set up 10 yards away.

"Fire!"

I pulled my gun from the holster. I aimed it down range and put that sight on the target. My nervous hand was flying all over the place. I took several deep breaths as I heard others taking their shots. But this was no race.

I placed the sight carefully over the target and then slowly squeezed the trigger.

The blast of the gun shocked me. But I squinted down range to see what had happened. A tiny black dot had appeared a ways to the left of the center of the target. And I knew in that moment why this left-ward drift had happened and how to correct for it.

A few more agents took their shots.

"Time for lunch, people!" the trainer shouted.

Over the next few days we would fill those clips and fire out all the bullets countless times. But I never departed from the basics I was being taught. Put that front sight on the target. Breathe. Carefully pull the trigger.

When it was all over, I was ranked just below a guy who had been an air marshal before joining the CIA. He still had to recertify here to go to Iraq. I had told the others I was the NSA'er on Day 3. By then they all knew me and liked me as a person, as well as respected me as competent in this training. And there were no hard feelings over the earlier jokes.

On Day 4, we practiced with perfect simulations of our Glocks that fired paint bullets. This was primarily to remove from us any psychological block from pulling our guns and then firing them on an actual human target. And those human targets were each other. We were wearing armor and goggles, but even so, those paint bullets hurt!

We practiced scenarios where we were in a car and ambushed. We practiced shooting from behind cover. And I was totally understanding why the other NSA'ers would be jealous that I got in on this training!

Day 5 saw us practicing firing various guns we may accidentally find in the field. I fired an AK-47. We fired massive shotguns. We fired rifles that could kill an elephant.

Lessons Learned

So how did a boy from Wisconsin, who somehow ended up training on weapons at a CIA facility, find success? In this particular case, the most important skill was simply to listen. There is a time and a place for personal initiative and promotion. There are times in which playing the rogue and the maverick will set you apart in ways that will help you get ahead both in life and in business. More often, however, the best course of action is to humbly listen and take orders from your superiors when you realize and accept that they know better than you. And knowing the difference only comes with wisdom and maturity.

Arriving In Iraq

And thus I got certified to carry a gun. Just two months later, on June 16, 2004, I was looking out the window of a plane and I saw below the unmistakable configuration of the Tigris and Euphrates rivers as they twist through Baghdad. I had seen it on maps while working the mission back in the US. Now I saw it below me with my own eyes.

At that time, with the war still on, we performed a landing maneuver in which the plane basically descends from a high altitude in a tight cork-screw toward the runway. This minimizes the chance that a bad guy with an anti-aircraft missile could be within range to get a shot on us. At the last second, as we spin toward the ground, the pilot turns us to land on the runway. We would take off in the same fashion.

I was on the ground at Baghdad International Airport (BIAP). But our plane had arrived too late in the day for me to be issued the Glock 9mm handgun I was certified on. The armory which would issue me my weapon would be open at 8:00 the following morning. And I'll admit, I was more than a little apprehensive to be in Iraq and yet be unarmed.

We were processed in and someone had made a mistake such that I was listed in the computers as a contractor. I was not a contractor. I was a federal employee. Because they had me listed as a contractor, they issued me a green badge, instead of the blue badge that a federal employee would wear. I am angry to this day that I walked around Iraq for three months, risking my life, while wearing a contractor's badge. Nothing against contractors, mind you. It's just that I wasn't one. I sure as hell wasn't being paid like one!

We were issued our body armor and helmets upon arrival, which we were told we needed to wear at all times while in Iraq, for our own protection. The body armor consisted of a vest which covered your front and back, inside of which were ceramic plates. The whole thing weighs about 30 pounds.

One Day In Baghdad

My onward travel to the base I actually served at would not be until the following afternoon. And so, I would spend the night at a facility in Baghdad near the airport. Shortly after my arrival there, we were all summoned to a central hall and told that, in the event of a security incident, there would be an alarm and we were all to report to this spot to be counted. I had arrived just in time to eat dinner in the main cafeteria. It was good food. Not that I needed it. I was about thirty pounds overweight and was hoping to both lose weight and get in shape during my three months in Iraq. Even so, one's first night in Iraq was no time to start a draconian program. So I ate everything in sight, which included burgers, French fries, and ice cream for dessert.

I was tired enough at 9:00PM that I decided it was time for sleep. My quarters were in a large room with about a dozen bunk beds—first come first serve. I took an available bottom bunk and sleep followed quickly.

Suddenly I was hearing a loud blaring noise! The fog of sleep was still blurring my brain as I saw guys getting out of their bunks and starting down the hall toward ... the central area. Oh my God! This was a security call.

Even just a week with that Glock had conditioned me in this crisis to put my hand toward a holster that wasn't there yet. My heart was racing as I thought through the potential that we were in an attack scenario and I was still defenseless.

In that moment, I felt utterly defeated to think that I was just hours into an experience slated to last for three months. As I quickly made my way down the hall toward the assembled group, I repeated to myself, "Three months, just three months."

We were told that an Army jeep had been found on the premises of BIAP with no soldiers in it, but blood all over the seats. We were therefore to stand in an alert mode until the military in charge of BIAP issued an all-clear.

The all-clear came about an hour later. I never did find out exactly what had happened in this incident. I was surprised that I fell asleep so quickly after this scare.

You can't really sleep in late when you're in a room with twenty other guys. There came a point when the sound of one, then three, then seven other men getting out of bed made it impossible to keep trying to catch more sleep.

The cafeteria offered a nice spread in the morning. Most important was the coffee my body was craving. I had a breakfast of scrambled eggs, sausage, and even a bowl of Lucky Charms to boot. One's second day in Iraq is also no time to start a serious diet.

I was just finishing my breakfast when I realized, it was finally 8:00AM! This meant that the armory would be open and I could get my sidearm.

There were already two guys in line when I arrived. Unfortunately, the one just before me faced a sadly typical problem within the government system. He had managed to get to Iraq. He was certainly supposed to be here. And I didn't really doubt that he had completed the necessary certifications to be issued the gun we were all required to wear here. But the man who issued guns at the armory simply had no record of him in his computer. And without a computer record, he had no authority to give him so much as a pea shooter.

Top Secrets

They attempted multiple searches for a record on various identifications. But no deal. The man finally left, understandably upset, with the plan to call his boss back in the States to see who screwed up and how to fix this problem.

My turn. And after watching that whole scene, I was now very nervous about whether I was in that computer. I was cringing as I told the man my Social Security Number. I heard him slapping keys on his computer. As I was about to despair that this could work, he smiled.

"Gotcha," he said.

Just then there was a low thud somewhere. I had both heard it and felt it.

"What was that?" I asked with alarm.

He looked up. "That was a mortar landing somewhere. Not very close though. Don't worry."

He hands me a plastic holster to slip on my belt. Next followed an empty magazine.

"Fill it up from the bowl behind you," he says.

I turn around and start fishing out cartridges and I'm filling my clip.

"And here's your Glock," he says. "Your site will have replacement bullets if you need them."

"Thank you," I said. "When do I get my M-4?"

"Only your boss at your site is authorized to issue you one of those. Good luck. How long are you in country?"

"Three months," I said.

He raises an eyebrow. "I won't be here when you cycle back to hand this thing in."

"Thanks for your help," I said.

I walk out of the building and feel already the heat of an Iraqi early summer starting to oppress the land. The flight to my main base was scheduled to leave at 3:00PM. Before then I had several free hours which would only be broken up by lunch.

I remember that as I walked from the armory back to the main building, I realized what day it was. It was June 17, 2004. It was two years to the day since I started at the National Security Agency. I was certainly far from Wisconsin.

I began the task of writing out a set of Romanian vocabulary cards. You see, my new girlfriend back in the States was a Romanian-American. And being a linguist, I could not be with someone without also wanting to express myself in her native language.

Lunch was fun. I had pizza and ice cream. And then I realized that my flight was not that far off. I had not really seen Baghdad. But at the end of one full day at this comfy little base, I was realizing that my life was about to change again. I had not come to Iraq to hang out in a villa at an airport near Baghdad.

Onward To My Base

3:00PM arrived and I was packing my bags onto a plane. It was a small plane, at least smaller than the one I flew in on. Besides the pilot there were seats for four, plus our luggage.

I learned that two of the four passengers on the plane were not going where I was, but would be dropped off at two of the three stops we would be making at sites outside Baghdad and in the direction of my base.

We took off exactly as I had landed. We corkscrewed to a safe altitude before turning in the direction we were to travel. (You'll understand that the location of my base outside Baghdad, even more than ten years later, is considered classified by the US Government.)

The man seated directly across from me sat looking casually out the window during the whole trip. He was about my height, but a slender bundle of muscle. Black hair, maybe Hispanic features but no discernible accent. And, despite what I told you about only getting rifles at your main site, he already had with him an M-4. And not just any M-4. This was a weapon he had personalized; he had it wrapped about with canvas straps on the barrel. This guy clearly used this gun. A lot. While in mid-flight I asked him where he was from originally.

Top Secrets

"Florida," he answered with a manner that seemed to imply that was the last question about his personal life he would entertain.

"I'm from Wisconsin," I said. "You'll be in [Location of my base] too, right?"

He smiled slightly and nodded. "You won't see me much."

I felt that the conversation had run its course. Despite what may have seemed like abruptness, he had never come off as rude. But in highly classified circles, I had come to understand that there are things and people I'm just not allowed to know too much about.

We were in another corkscrew. And after a maneuver I was becoming familiar with, we had landed in [a place I can't name].

One of us got off along with her luggage and soon we were back in the air. A while later, there was another stop to deliver supplies and personnel.

Our last stop before [my base] was [yet another place I can't name], where we dropped off some cargo for a site there. Soon we were in the air again and a short time later, on the ground in [my base].

Arriving At My Base

A large black Mercedes pulls up to the airport. Out step two men, both walls of muscle, wearing body armor and helmets and carrying M-4 assault rifles.

"You Massey?" one of them says.

"Yes, sir."

"Okay, Massey, here's how it works. You're going to be sitting directly behind me while I drive. I need you to be in charge of that side of the car. If I tell you to abandon the vehicle or give you a target to open fire on, you have to do exactly what I say. Is that understood?"

"Yes, sir," I say, through a frog in my throat.

He slaps an M-4 to my chest. "This is yours and it stays on safety unless I tell you otherwise. You know how to use this, right?"

I had not touched one for two months. But the muscle memory I got at my CIA training kicked in. I took the gun and confirmed the safety status of the weapon. "I'm set."

It did occur to me, however, that I had been explicitly told that I could only be issued one of these by my boss at my base. In that moment I just assumed that the situation on the ground superseded such rules.

The ride from the airport to our base took about a half an hour. Never in my life had I felt such stress as we made our way through the streets of [the city I can't name]. I had no idea exactly where we were headed. When finally we turned off a major street and were moving up a long driveway, I knew we were out of the immediate danger of driving in the city.

We pulled up to a stately three story villa. The men conducting my ride began to laugh after we arrived. I learned that making the new guy believe the ride from the airport was a complete peril constituted a type of hazing ritual.

I knew my supervisor's name was Jim and that he would greet me upon my arrival. A tall and muscular man approached me. I would later learn that he was a semi-professional body builder earlier in life.

"You're Keith?" he asked, offering his hand.
"Jim?" I said, shaking.
"Good to meet you. Let me get your bag."
He picked up my large suitcase as if it were a purse and started up the driveway. I followed, struggling with my smaller duffle bag.

Our base circled the massive villa, which served as the eating spaces of all the personnel and the living spaces of some of the officers stationed there. We had a twenty-foot tall concrete wall around the entire compound. My own quarters were in a white trailer in a valley perhaps 30 feet lower in elevation than the main villa. My trailer had sand bags atop the roof and all along the walls outside by my bed. This was presumably to protect the occupant from a mortar attack while sleeping.

My trailer contained a bed, a lounge chair, and a TV, connected via satellite to a number of channels. My TV was also hooked up to a DVD player. We had a library of movies in the main house, many of them bootlegs, that I took little advantage of, owing to my fitness plan which I will describe below.

We had arrived after the dinner hour. Jim showed me the snack area of the kitchen in the main house. I grabbed some bags of chips to tide me over until the next morning.

The sun had set. I spent some time watching TV in my quarters and had eaten the chips but still felt hungry. After meticulously locking my quarters (as I was told I had to do for security reasons), I went back to the main house and grabbed an Eskimo Pie from the freezer. And I further resolved that, starting the next day, ice cream must not be an everyday occurrence.

Three Moons In Iraq

On my way back to my trailer, I stopped at the top of the flight of stairs leading down toward the level of my quarters. I looked into the black night. There I saw just the faintest sliver of a moon, soon to vanish before the new moon to follow. And I knew in that moment that I would watch three lunar cycles before I left this place.

Three moons. Three months. And every night, as I looked at the cycles of the moon, I knew where I stood in the time left of this deployment.

(In the appendix to this book, I describe in detail my research into three month long bursts of exertion and how you can use this program for personal accomplishment.)

Life In Iraq

My typical day started at 4:00AM. I would always be lights out by 8:00PM the previous night to ensure eight hours of sleep before that wake up time. Someone at the NSA, whom I very much respect, had told me before my departure that the best way to survive deployments is to make sure you plan your day around no less than eight hours of sleep a night. And the reason is two-fold. For starters, you will simply be sharper and healthier by getting the appropriate amount of sleep. But secondly, sleep has a way of fast forwarding the night. And a good night's sleep means fewer hours awake of waiting to come home.

At 4:00AM I went to the villa and I made a pot of coffee and I drank a cup. Then I went and worked out for an hour on exercise equipment we had on base. I would eat breakfast at 6:00AM and my boss and I started work at 6:30.

We would typically take a half hour lunch break at noon. And we would finish work at 6:00PM, an eleven hour work day. At that point we would go to the main house for the evening meal. And, as I have said, I personally would be lights out at 8:00PM to start the cycle over again.

With just an hour after dinner before I would go to sleep, I would study Romanian vocabulary for a bit each night. I also watched a little TV. There was the Summer Olympics in Athens in 2004. I recall watching the US Team enter during the opening ceremonies. Proud of my country, and risking my life working for her in that moment, I shed copious tears expressing a wide range of emotions.

June turned into July. On July 4th, the base managed to get beers and steaks for us to have for an Independence Day celebration. I did not change my sleep routine for the party, but I did enjoy the indulgence before I turned in.

Under Attack

When I went to Iraq, I was understandably apprehensive about the possibility of some attack. The insurgency was on the rise at that time. And about a month after I arrived, I truly experienced war.

Top Secrets

In those kinds of temperatures (well over a hundred every day during the summer there), you need to be constantly rehydrating. And, as a result, you are also constantly needing to urinate. I had just stepped outside my work building to head for the restroom when I suddenly heard the sound of someone, I presumed at the main house, slamming a door unnecessarily hard. My deep and visceral reaction at hearing this door slam so loudly was anger. Why does someone need to slam a door like that? I continued toward the bathroom and I heard it again. And anger surged within me. There was no rational cause for slamming a door in that fashion!

And then I saw the most curious thing. It was an object, spinning end over end through the air. It landed outside our base by a distance. And as it did, I heard, not a door slam, but a massive explosion. And then I saw another one! It spins end over end and lands beyond our wall. I now hear and feel the shock wave of an explosion.

And then I realized. These are mortars! I ran as fast as I could toward a building called the FEBR

(Federally Evaluated Blast Resistant). Some of the officers on base were lucky enough to work inside it all day, while I was in a trailer with sandbags on the roof. The people inside were so insulated that they didn't even hear the sounds.

Our security detail made us all sit in place for a period of time until they gave the all-clear. The mortar attack was clearly directed at our base, but there are so many variables, wind speed, etc, that they missed us. What I was hearing as a door slamming were mortars in the attack. The human body makes sense of new sensations by turning them into things that are familiar. I had never heard an explosion so loud as a mortar. Until I saw it, that thing was just an irrationally loud noise.

The fact is, we had all tended to get a little lazy about security protocols. I mean, I had been issued a helmet and body armor in Baghdad. Was I wearing them when that attack happened? Nope. And a small shift in wind between me and the place from which that mortar was launched could have dropped it right next to me. Those protections would then have possibly saved my life, if I had been wearing them. As it is, I was just lucky I didn't need those items, which were sitting vainly in my quarters, while I was under attack.

After that incident, many people, myself included, began wearing our protective gear regularly. But, I'll be honest, after some days, everyone, myself included, got lazy again!

The Second Attack

Eleven days after the first attack, I was sitting in my work station with my boss. And we heard a deafening boom. Within a second this time, I was saying, that's a mortar attack! We bolted from our seats and out the door.

While we ordinarily locked our classified work spaces when we left them, we were under orders to not worry about that when our lives were in danger. But the sheer force of habit made us risk our lives that day. As we hurried from our work space, under attack, we turned and I began to secure the lock on the door. We heard two more horribly loud explosions.

I had just finished locking the door when my boss suddenly screams, "What are we doing! Forget the lock!" We run toward the FEBR and arrive safely inside.

It was determined that, once again, our base was clearly the intended target but that all the mortars had fallen just outside our main wall. Interestingly, in addition to once again wearing all the protective gear, people began talking about how the second attack, coming 11 days after the first, was an indication of the enemy's plan. Word was being spread on base that the enemy clearly attacks us every eleven days!

I did not embrace that logic, but I will admit that, on the "Eleventh Day" after the second attack, I was wearing my protective gear again with the rest, just in case. The day passed without incident. And there would be no further attack on my base while I was there.

Taking A PQE In Iraq

July turned into August.

While I was in Iraq, the next PQE cycle arrived. As I described above, if I were to pass this test, it would mean a significant pay increase.

My boss was an authorized proctor to administer the PQE test to me at a field site such as Iraq. But the test took two hours. And he told me that our important mission (a large part of which was directed at force protection of US soldiers) really could not allow me to take two hours off from our normal day. So he proposed to me the following compromise. I could take this test, but I would have to put in two hours of work prior to our normal 6:30AM start time. Then, at the beginning of our work day, he would proctor the two hour test and we would finish the day normally.

It was a practical, reasonable, and charitable solution to the problem of administering a PQE test to a candidate in a war zone. But it was not lost on me just how much more of a hardship I would be facing on this test compared with my colleagues back at the NSA headquarters. When I took such tests back there, the time for the test was given to me as part of my work day! Not to mention the fact that I would be taking a PQE under the potential threat of a mortar attack.

The night before the test, I went to sleep at my normal 8:00PM. I got up at four and went in to work. After two hours, I took a break and went to breakfast. My boss and I returned and he set up the test for me. For the next two hours I worked at the thing.

This final PQE test was a listening passage of a classified artifact. At the half way point, I was getting pretty optimistic. I had already finished my transcription. I had a full hour remaining to review my work. Maybe it was the fact that I had been working a listening mission for some time now. I listened over and over again and I could not find anything further to change in my transcription.

I had passed a *graphic* PQE with honors. And I was beginning to dare to hope that I may not only have *passed* this current test, but even passed it with honors as well. Knowing the long and arduous road I had faced previously with listening tests, you can imagine my excitement.

The Results Come In

About a week later, I learned that the results were in, because I had been emailing with people back at NSA headquarters who knew their scores. So I emailed the field site liaison, telling her that I was anxious to know my results as soon as they were available. I mean, I was in Iraq, for God's sake. If you have good news for me, please let me know!

I emailed her on Friday morning her time, begging for the news, one way or another. An indicator in our email server told me she was at work that day. And I knew that she had my results. No response.

When I sent a follow-up email on Monday morning, I got an auto-reply, "I'm on vacation for a week!"

I was in Iraq. I had a strong suspicion that I had passed that test, which was so important to me. And now I had to wait an entire week. And when you worry that your life could end in an instant from a mortar attack, a week to hear good news is an eternity.

A week later, I finally got an email from her informing me that I had passed that test. In fact, as I suspected, I had passed it with honors. I was simultaneously elated and enraged. This news would have been a salve to my soul when she received it a week earlier and did not forward it to me in a timely manner.

I wrote a strongly worded email response, telling her how I felt about the treatment I had received. My boss told me that before I sent it he wanted to have a look at it. When he had done so, he told me that he had hoped writing the message helped me vent some energy, but that I should now delete it and just move on.

And I realized he was right. The negative emotions I was feeling were my own. They were because of where I was. Even though I think she should have told me the news as soon as she had it, I understand that sitting in a cubicle in the US does not allow one to fully understand the trials going on elsewhere. Letting it go, forgiving her, gave me peace to press forward.

End Of The Deployment

August finally turned into September. Three moons had come and gone. I had lost thirty pounds. I had passed the final PQE. I flew away. And I had hoped I could have a little bit of vacation before I had to go back to full time work at the NSA. But it turned out that the fall of 2004 was surging with concerns of potential attacks. And I was called back immediately to the NSA, to begin work at the Counter-Terrorism Office there.

Lessons Learned

I have some regrets about my time in Iraq. About a month into my stay, the rising security concerns prompted a significant military augment to our base. They brought in a unit of National Guard Soldiers who were stationed with us for protection. I got to know these guys and really liked them. They lived in the main house with the other officers (and these soldiers did not officially know what we were, but they must have been able to conclude). When some of them had free time in the evening, they would ask me over dinner to join them in a game of Risk. I was so locked into the schedule I have described to you—lights out at eight, work out at four, work, repeat—that I continually declined the invitation for that evening, but I assured them I would eventually play a game with them.

When I was about to fly back to Baghdad and then onward to home, the National Guard guys and I were waiting at the airport. One of them said, "Hey, we never got you into a game of Risk."

And I felt a deep sadness to think that I wished I had played even one game with those guys and now it was too late. In my own strategy to survive that experience, I had become so closed off. I wish I had a few weeks back before my departure. I would decide that I didn't need to go to sleep every night at 8:00 and work out at 4:00. I would decide that memories built with those men were more important than my rigid schedule.

People matter. I missed the chance to experience genuine human connections because I was self-absorbed in my schedule and weight loss goals. All the weight I lost in my workout regimen would eventually go back on. But the time I could have spent with my friends in Iraq was lost forever.

Our professional lives and the drive to succeed there will frequently make demands on our families that seem in each individual instance to be necessary sacrifices for advancement. But we need to make sure that work doesn't win every time all the way until we lose something far more valuable than the next promotion.

Life is precious and life is short. I had never before been in a situation in which I might reasonably face the end of my life. On the evenings after the mortar attacks, people would say things like, "We could have been killed today." And the saddest thing about it is just how fast we normalize and fall back into denial regarding the fragility of our human condition.

Every day as I commute now to work, there is the potential danger that, no matter how careful *I* am, something could happen outside my control that could change or end my life or the life of my loved ones.

There is a Medieval Latin proverb:

Memento mori

Remember that you have to die.

This might strike us moderns as unnecessarily morbid. But the wisdom of it is simple. You are going to die. So live your life in the fullness of expressed love to those around you, knowing that

Top Secrets

every day is a gift and a chance that will never come back to you.

CHAPTER THREE: INSIDE THE NSA (2004-2006)

In the fall of 2004, I was back from Iraq. I had achieved full professionalization as an Arabic linguist at the NSA. Not surprisingly, I was assigned to the Office of Counter-Terrorism. I'll be honest, the dream of working in that office was the primary reason I joined the NSA. And so, I settled back into life in the United States. I had the deep privilege of working with the best minds in the industry, serving our country in this most critical of areas.

My last two years at the NSA were no less eventful than the first two. I earned the coveted role of QC status in that prestigious office. I would go on another deployment during those last two years. But unfortunately, by the nature of the work

I was doing and the office in which I was doing it, I can say very little about those final two years. I can report that I was promoted to Grade 13 as a result of my accomplishments. But otherwise, all I can say is that I spent my final two years at the National Security Agency doing what Arabic linguists do at the NSA.

I will, however, share an anecdote of an intelligence "failure" that I was an instrumental part of. The NSA approved the following account as being stripped enough of Top Secret details to be publishable as unclassified.

Some Saturday at the NSA

You'll be relieved, I hope, to learn that Arabic linguists at the NSA are always on the job at the Counterterrorism Office. While many people work a traditional Monday to Friday, 9 to 5 schedule, there are people assigned to the night shift and weekends such that the mission is never truly turned off. And so it happened that I, one Saturday, was at work. But I had risen in responsibility enough that I had the authority to forward a piece of intelligence for official reporting. And there was something in our intelligence that I decided to report to our policy makers.

So, here's the issue. In this "piece" of intelligence, someone had communicated something potentially worrisome. I knew from my experience in Iraq that a particular word in the "piece" was a known cover-term for an attack.

Cover-Terms

Maybe you're not familiar with the concept of a "cover-term." Let's imagine you and I want to talk on the phone and plan a surprise birthday party for your spouse. But we worry that he may overhear us.

So, to keep our little surprise party a secret, you and I come up with a "cover-term" in advance. Every time I say, "Hey, let's talk about our upcoming 'fishing trip'," it's really a conversation about the surprise party.

"Have you made any arrangements for the 'fishing trip'," I ask.
"Yeah, I've already scoped out the 'fishing spot'."

Except "fishing spot" means "restaurant" by another pre-arranged cover-term.

So, the piece contained a well-known, even openly published, cover-term for "attack."

And I decided, out of an abundance of caution, that the "piece" needed to be reported.

Now, I haven't yet explained the whole "reporting" process. The NSA takes intercepted communications and turns them into intelligence reports. These reports go out via the classified network to various intelligence consumers. If it's terrorism related, for instance, you can imagine that the White House is an automatic recipient of the report.

Having been in a war zone, I would want to know if there is even a hint of a possibility of a rumor of danger out there before I step outside my door. So, for me, this was a no-brainer. Of course we issue a report. And that report will contain the necessary caveats. We'll explain in the report that this "word," while it is a well-known cover-term, may be literally true. Based on my opinion, we issued this report. And it turned out that, in this case, a cigar *was* just a cigar.

Monday Morning Quarterbacks

I had just opened my email, when my boss approached my cubicle.

"Dr. Massey?"

"Yes?"

"You've been summoned to attend the Director's morning briefing at 9:00AM. They expect you and the reporter to explain that report that went out."

I knew immediately what report she must be talking about. And I felt my blood pressure surge thirty degrees. "What's going on?"

"One of our embassies shut down because of that report. They worried that they might be the target."

"So?" I asked. "Maybe that was a good idea."

"The Intelligence forces there investigated the matter. And it turns out…"

A cigar was just a cigar.

Our Ambassador was angry. The RSO (Regional Security Officer at the Embassy) was even calling the report "reckless." The CIA was saying the report was unnecessarily "sensationalist."

And now I had to explain to the Director of the NSA himself why I wanted to send out that report.

Knowing now that "a cigar was just a cigar," the piece suddenly did seem mundane. In light of this information, it seemed obvious to me after the fact that the piece had not been talking about an attack at all, but was talking only about a real cigar.

But obviously hindsight is 20/20.

I seemed to be in trouble. All I could do was explain why I did what I did.

**

The reporter and I sat at a large table in a room that seemed slightly too small for the furniture. The walls were covered with historical scenes and also maps of regions in Afghanistan and Iraq that were quite current in their importance. Other people entered slowly and took seats. They greeted one another with a relaxation that told me they weren't there to explain their actions to a man who reported directly to the President. Most were military officers, and high ranks at that. A few others were well dressed civilians who looked to be about fourteen places up the management chain from me.

I had not expected to be summoned to a meeting with the Director of the NSA that day and so I was dressed in my normal white dress shirt and khaki slacks. I wished I at least had a tie to throw on. But no such luck.

Everyone stood and so, I did as well. In walked the Four Star General Director of the National Security Agency. He's enjoying a well-deserved retirement now after decades of distinguished service to our nation. But that morning, he had called me on the carpet to explain why the CIA and State Department were crying foul over the report I wanted to send out.

He told everyone to take their seats and I found myself listening to his regular morning briefing. A colonel gave a report about optimizing resources, followed by another person talking about leveraging assets. I was starting to wonder if I was really supposed to be there at all. Finally, the

Director puts his finger on the agenda in front of him.

"Alright, last order of business," he says, and turns to us. "You two issued that report that's got everyone so mad at the NSA. I'd like you to please explain everything that went into your decision to send out that report."

The disapproving eyes of an entire room tore into us like laser beams.

As calmly as we could, we explained that the piece included a clear use of a known cover-term. We also pointed out that the final report we issued did remind readers that there was no way to know for certain if this was a cover-term or an innocent event. And we would always err on the side of caution and put the information out in case someone else had a different piece of the puzzle.

And I have to add, by the way, I do take full responsibility for the decision to release that report, right or wrong. But that reporter was being very loyal to stand beside me.

Top Secrets

The Director had sat and listened to us carefully. "And if you had this to do over again?"

"General," the reporter said. "We issued that report based on the information we had at the time. And I personally would do it all over again, even if it means I lose my job."

The general smiled. "That's good enough for me. I'll push back and tell the other agencies that the NSA stands by its report. Just because it's proven wrong doesn't mean it wasn't the right thing to do at the time."

I felt as if a ton of bricks were lifted from my shoulders.

***

I was getting ready to call it a day when a finely suited man approached my cubicle. I recognized him from the meeting earlier.

"The Director asked me to deliver something to you," he said, stretching out his hand.

I took from him a small bronze coin and I knew from a glance what I was holding. "Presented by the Director" was engraved around one side. This was a cherished memento of my briefing to the very head of the NSA. Higher officers give their subordinates coins in recognition of various achievements.

In military circles, when a group of people gather for a celebration, frequently each person presents the highest ranked coin they hold. The holder of the lowest ranked coin has to pay for the drinks. The Director of the NSA is a Four Star General. It is unlikely that I would ever have to buy another drink in a military gathering.

Lessons Learned

What would have happened if I had not insisted on releasing this report? Well, in this particular case, absolutely nothing. Meaning, no one would have been hurt because it turned out that the "piece" wasn't truly a threat.

But in another world, this "piece" could have mattered. And unreported, lives could have been lost. Even though it wasn't a threat, I still could have found myself conflicted over time about the risk I took in not reporting it. I did what, in my conscience, I had to do.

And that's the real lesson. We all have to conduct ourselves in our personal and professional lives in a manner that we can live with long term. Don't get me wrong, there are many ways I have failed in my personal and professional conduct. I take responsibility for that.

I will always err on the side of caution, even when I strongly suspect that it is an error. Because I will not be able to defend a loss I could have prevented by "playing it safe."

There is also a lesson here in the burden of responsibility that comes with being a leader. To be effective, you will have to frequently make decisions that others will question based on how matters turn out.

There is an analogy I use to push back against such retrospective re-evaluation of decisions. Imagine you are out hunting. You are trying to bag a deer (hey, I'm from Wisconsin, so this analogy might trend rustic). This particular area is so well-known to be teeming with deer that there are also lots of other hunters around. Suddenly, you see about 10 yards away, there is a bush that is rustling. Is it a deer? You raise your rifle and point it toward the bush. The bush continues to rustle vigorously. So here's the thing. You cannot see what is in that bush. Based on everything you know, it is either a deer or a hunter. And so, should you take the shot?

Not knowing what is in the bush, you hesitate. Just then, you watch a glorious twelve point buck bolt from the bush. Before you can react, he has vanished into the woods.

So now the question is—were you, in retrospect, wrong to *not* take the shot? The answer, of course, is that you did the right thing at the time. Just because you later found out that the rustling was caused by a deer does not mean that shooting blindly into a bush that might as easily have hosted a human was a responsible choice.

But you will meet people who will indeed retroactively second-guess your decisions based on the outcome. And the burden of leadership is that all you can do is defend your decisions based on the data you had and move forward.

My decision to release that report was also based on a desire that the information be available when it might be able to make a difference. Colin Powell, a man who certainly knows the burden of leadership, describes what he terms the 40-70 Formula regarding information and decision making. He states that a decision based on less than 40% of the necessary information runs the serious risk of being in error. At the same time, a decision that waits until more than 70% of the necessary information arrives will likely not be timely enough to be effective. And that means that leaders must routinely make decisions based on less confirmational data than they would have preferred in order to be successful in the fast changing realm of everything from the battlefield to the business world.

My Career at the NSA Comes To An End

Prior to going to Iraq, I had worked two years at the NSA. I would work two more, remaining at the Office of Counter-Terrorism for the duration of my time there.

I married my wife Adriana at the end of 2004, just after I got back from Iraq. She had a job teaching Spanish in New Jersey, making more money than I was as a Top Secret agent. We decided to continue working our jobs and seeing each other on weekends.

As 2006 was starting I made the decision that I was ready to move on. My wife could not have found a job making as much money as she was earning if she quit her job and moved to my area. And I saw that I could get a teaching job for not much less than I was making at the National Security Agency. We would also then have our summers free to share our love of travel. And so it happened that I left the NSA in July of 2006 and became a Latin teacher in New Jersey.

I am honored to have had the opportunity to serve my country using my particular talents during that period of time. And I will always be grateful for the life lessons I learned while serving at the NSA. I will share in Part Two of this book applications from specific disciplines within the intelligence community to maximize your own personal and professional success.

CHAPTER FOUR:
HOW I GOT MY MEDAL

I learned that, after my departure from the NSA, a medal had been created which acknowledged service in war zones performed by civilian federal employees.

The **Global War on Terrorism Civilian Service Medal** is to be issued to employees satisfying the following criteria:

* 30 or more consecutive days in a field of operation. (I satisfied that times three.)
* Must have worked in direct support of the Coalition efforts. (I did, though I can't say much more about it than that.)
* Must also have been a federal employee during this service, not a private contractor. (Despite the

color of my badge in Iraq, I really was a federal employee while there.)

The regulations for the medal did also explicitly state that the medal is to be issued to personnel who have subsequently left federal employment. And the medal was retroactive for anyone qualifying, all the way back to September 11, 2001.

Even though I was now a mild-mannered Latin teacher at a public high school, I was fully qualified to have this medal issued to me.

And I'll admit, I wanted my medal. A federal level medal is a big deal. I'm qualified for it and, darn it, I deserve it.

But here's the catch. Just because you qualify, doesn't mean you have been automatically issued the medal. It still has to be officially issued to you by a division of the Department of Defense qualified to issue it. And I was now outside the NSA.

I still have friends on the inside, however, with whom I maintain email contact. So I wrote to a fellow that had been in Iraq after me, asking if he knew about this medal. I learned that he and everyone he knew that qualified for the medal had already been issued the thing! This seemed like great news, because if they got it, then I'm going to get it too, right? So, I asked him to please send a message inside the NSA to the people who issued him the medal, asking how a former employee goes about getting the medal issued to them.

I received no response for some time and I wrote back and learned that he had sent the message up the chain of command and received no reply as yet. But he told me he would write again to see what had happened on the matter.

And what followed was a frustrating period of several months in which more than one person inside the NSA tried to get this matter addressed, and no one apparently could succeed.

I suspected what might be going on. The issuing of that medal actually does require someone within management filling out a form, writing a formal letter or whatnot, and sending it somewhere. In other words, it requires some effort on their part. And the reality was that management really has no incentive whatsoever to expend effort on a former employee.

Yes, out of sheer justice I had earned the medal and should therefore have it issued to me. But a manager gets something out of issuing a medal to a current employee. The gratitude the recipient has will translate into loyalty and performance. But a former employee is a different matter. Also, as a former employee, I had no way to directly contact the managers inside who might be able to resolve the situation.

I had started my little campaign in March of 2011. I wrote to people inside the NSA from time to time but for almost a year I got nowhere. I recounted this saga to a woman at my Church in February of 2012 and she told me that this was precisely the kind of thing that one needs to write their congressman about. She informed me that members of Congress have staff specifically designated to assist constituents who need help cutting through governmental red tape.

Following her advice, I wrote the office of Rodney Frelinghuysen, my Representative in New Jersey, explaining the situation and asking if the

Congressman could help. I received a prompt reply from a staffer in his office requesting some documentation from me describing the situation in full detail. I sent it in and hoped that perhaps finally something might happen.

About a week later, I got a call on my cell phone. It was someone from the NSA telling me that they were very sorry that the Global War on Terrorism Civilian Service Medal had never been issued to me and that it had now been issued immediately. Furthermore, the woman on the phone told me that they would be mailing the hard copy of the medal to me, but the Certificate itself would follow later after receiving the appropriate signature.

I told her that I didn't need anyone to buy the hard copy of the medal for me. I knew where one could buy it online, I only needed it officially issued.

She repeated that it had just been officially issued and that they really were going to be mailing me the medal itself, she just needed to confirm my mailing address. I confirmed the information.

The next day, I came home and found a FedEx package by my door. They had over-nighted the medal to me!

I did learn later that a friend inside the NSA felt he was getting close to getting my situation resolved, but the manner in which the NSA acted, one week after the Congressman got on the case, told me who finally lit a fire under them.

I called the Congressman's office and conveyed my gratitude for his efforts on my behalf. And then, to my surprise, a few days later I received a signed letter from him, thanking *me* for my service. Rep. Rodney Frelinghuysen is a class act and I appreciate his letter as much as the medal itself.

The Certificate and the Congressman's letter hang in my study. I didn't go to Iraq to earn a medal. Indeed, it didn't exist yet when I went. But I'll admit, this token of appreciation is a special memento of my time of service there.

Lessons Learned

In retrospect, the almost year I spent trying and failing to get that medal issued to me was a lesson in proactivity versus passivity. Sending a message to someone else, who had no true interest in furthering my cause, asking them to please forward my request to someone else inside the NSA, who equally had no true interest in furthering my cause, was a waste of time and energy. Most importantly, it was lazy on *my* part.

I needed to diagnose the true problem earlier and change my tactic. As I described above, no one on the inside gets anything from me receiving that medal. Once I realized the medal wasn't coming my way, and a month should have been sufficient for that conclusion, I needed to change my approach. But I didn't. I continued to passively write back to the same people, asking them to please just try again. I don't blame any of them or even the management chain inside the NSA for my failure to get the situation resolved.

Another takeaway is that sometimes there are situations you really can't solve on your own. You need help. And knowing you need help and then finding the best sources for help will be crucial to resolving your problem. In this particular case, the information I needed came through networking. I didn't know that my Congressman could be of such important assistance. And the problem was not solved until I shared with another person the details of my situation and then benefited from the knowledge of my wider social network.

Part Two: Using Lessons from Intelligence Analysis for Personal and Professional Success

Chapter Five: Human Intelligence (HUMINT)

Definition of HUMINT

Human Intelligence is intelligence gathered by people interacting with other people. Now, that interaction is not always a mutual sharing. For instance, if a spy somewhere manages to be sitting at a restaurant in the booth next to an intelligence target, and she overhears the target say something important, that is intelligence gathered by a person from a person. It's Human Intelligence. But, generally speaking, HUMINT involves someone sharing information directly with another person. And the person sharing the secret is generally doing so with a motive. Frequently the motive is money.

Who Conducts HUMINT?

Most HUMINT in the United States Intelligence Community is conducted by the CIA. The fact that they have clandestine agents all over the world is hardly a secret, since you can apply to be a clandestine agent right on their website![3] And the job of such clandestine agents is to obtain information of intelligence value from other people. Theoretically it does not matter who the people are from which they glean their

---

[3] The CIA conducts HUMINT with its "Directorate of Operations (Formerly known as the Clandestine Service)."
https://www.cia.gov/careers/opportunities/clandestine/index.html

information. The only thing that matters is whether it has intelligence value. In other words, a diplomat from country A stationed in country B obviously knows things policy makers in the United States would like to learn. But if that diplomat talks too openly about state secrets when he's had a few too many to drink, his butler might be the source of valuable intelligence as well!

While Human Intelligence is conducted primarily and formally by the CIA, there are other government agencies that do Human Intelligence in an unofficial capacity all the time. If a US diplomat, an employee of the State Department, is at a dinner in the country of his or her posting, and they learn something that may be of intelligence value, they are obligated to report such information.

What are the most important issues in HUMINT?

By definition, HUMINT is information one person wants another person to have. The problem is, there are multiple motivations one could have for sharing information. One of them may indeed be a desire to mislead! In fact, there have been cases in the history of espionage in which a spy has told another spy true information merely to establish credibility for a long term plan to do substantial damage at a later date with misinformation.[4]

The point is, whenever a spy learns information from an asset, all we really know is that the asset wants the spy to have that info. We technically know nothing about the credibility of the information itself.

We all go through our day under what is known as the "Truth Bias." In other words, virtually everything people say to you all day long is true. And, for that reason, we receive information and incorporate it into our daily plans assuming it is true unless we learn otherwise.

---

[4] A notorious example of this is the so-called "Double Cross System" run by British Intelligence during WWII. Captured German agents who agreed to collaborate were fed legitimate information to report back so that eventual misinformation would be more readily believed. This plan is credited with the success of the D-Day Landing. See, *Double Cross: The True Story of the D-Day Spies*, by Ben Macintyre (New York: 2012).

I mean, imagine if you tried to function under the complete opposite of the truth bias. If everything you heard from everyone in your life was assumed to be a lie unless you learned otherwise, you would lose your mind in the exhaustion of chasing down confirmation of the information around you.

The problem for HUMINT is that we sometimes take in this information without subjecting it to appropriate scrutiny. In the category of HUMINT, we should be much more discriminating about the potential for misinformation than in our day-to-day lives. And yet, in the history of espionage, credence has sometimes been given to information despite obvious red flags.

Perhaps the most famous recent example of an Intelligence failure connected to the "Truth Bias" is the misplaced credence that was given to the Intelligence source known as "Curveball." This man, Rafid Ahmed Alwan, had made claims to German Intelligence regarding the Chemical Weapons capabilities of the Saddam Hussein regime in order to gain asylum and permanent residency there.5 Information he supplied eventually was reported by Secretary of State Colin Powell to the UN in the lead up to the Iraq War.

CIA reports contain an automatic caveat at the end, to the effect that whatever information this report contains may have been provided with the intention to "deceive or mislead." Hopefully the presence of this caveat leads policy makers to take the information provided for exactly what it might be worth—which could be, in some cases, a grain of salt.

One final anecdotal comment. As of the time I left the NSA, CIA reports that I saw WERE BEING RELEASED IN ALL CAPS! Now, maybe they were only in all caps in the systems I had access to. Maybe, like NSA reports, they were actually released to policy makers in a nice professional office style.

But if all readers of these reports were seeing them in all caps like I was, that is a potential

---

[5] "Iraq war source's name revealed." *BBC News*, November 2, 2007. http://news.bbc.co.uk/2/hi/middle_east/7075501.stm

problem. Anything written in all caps seems to scream at you. I hope that the effect of all caps did not result in a bias wherein the font itself seemed to imply urgency.

Circular Reporting

A final point analysts have to remember when weighing the veracity of HUMINT, and in fact this applies to other disciplines within the Intelligence Community as well, is the possibility of what is known as circular reporting. This is also known as False Confirmation. Multiple sources all stating the same information are not necessarily independent voices.

For instance, if you told all your friends a story, and they all went and told the story to their spouses, the fact that the story was related by a number of different people does not make it more reliable. It came from a single source.

Circular Reporting is precisely what makes false rumors seem credible. Once the rumor really takes off, you are hearing it from multiple, seemingly unconnected, sources. You think to yourself, that's the third person I've heard that news from today. It must be true. But that false rumor could have started with one source, who intentionally fed misinformation to someone, knowing it would take off like wildfire.

Lessons Learned

We all go through our lives keeping our sanity with the Truth Bias. But in both our personal and professional lives, the lessons learned from the practice and failures of HUMINT in the world of espionage should give us pause to consider the veracity of the information around us.

Rather than react to all the information we receive as if it were necessarily true, we should receive it through the following filter:

"Someone has just told me something because they wanted me to hear it."

And before we make decisions based on that information, we should consider all of the possible motives for that information exchange.

It remains probable that people who tell you things are telling you what they think is the truth.

But the lesson of HUMINT is that we should be open to other possibilities. We should break out of the Truth Bias, reacting to all information we hear as if it is, by the hearing, therefore true.

For instance, I've learned in life to just smile and nod whenever anyone tells me about their marriage. Whether they are telling me it's perfect or horrible, all they are telling me is what they want me to hear. It does not necessarily have anything to do with reality.

It is equally important to keep in mind that someone may tell you something, legitimately believing the information to be true, when it's not. The take away from HUMINT is that information we receive from another person is just that—information. The best way to make decisions for our personal and professional lives is to collect as much information as possible, even and especially information that contradicts other sources, so that we can weigh all the facts.

And when collecting and weighing information for important decisions in your life, always consider the possibility that an abundance of evidence for one position may have actually come from a single source.

Applications for your Organization

A knowledge of how nations conduct HUMINT has profound implications for what you should assume could be operative within Business Espionage as well. Extraction of actionable intelligence by the use of human agents could take several forms. Chief among them will always be either the bribery or extortion of one of your current employees with access to sensitive information. Also in the realm of possibility could be undercover agents of a competitor—people who attempt to secure employment and thereby gain access to sensitive information. Another way to gain access to your secrets could take the form of stealing documents or equipment from one of your employees outside of your organization's walls—in their homes or while on a business trip.

Important responses to all these situations include maintaining the most prudent limitations on who within your organization has access to your most sensitive information, coupled with strenuous password protection of all materials containing it.

When vetting people for a security clearance, the Intelligence Agencies are always looking for familial or professional ties to potentially hostile entities. So, for instance, if you are a naturalized citizen with a brother who is a sommelier in France, there's no reason to doubt your loyalty. If, however, you have a sister who is an employee of the Egyptian General Intelligence (EGI), you will likely never receive a Top Secret clearance.

Corporations should be vetting potential (and current) employees by investigating online conduct, but also such connections to competitors as could potentially be ascertained in social media. Remember that counter intelligence measures admit that we can never guarantee we're totally safe, but we should at least make our adversaries work overtime to achieve anything against us.

CHAPTER SIX: SIGNALS INTELLIGENCE (SIGINT)

Definition of SIGINT

Signals Intelligence (SIGINT) involves the interception of electronic signals. Frequently, these signals include personal communication of some type. But not always. For example, if some belligerent country, such as North Korea, attempts to launch a three stage ICBM, you can bet the US is trying to intercept the telemetry data that missile is sending home. And the North Koreans know that. So they encrypt those signals the best they can. And hopefully the US has the skills to both intercept that data and decrypt it. But such data is not, as it were, personal communication.

Within the Intelligence Community, intercepted signals that involve communication are called COMINT (Communications Intelligence). Signals of more technical data, such as the telemetry of the missile described above, are called ELINT (Electronic Intelligence).

But since the vast majority of Signals Intelligence sent to US policy makers is, technically, COMINT, people frequently just use the term SIGINT to mean personal communications as well. And that's the term I will use.

Who Conducts SIGINT?

The US Agency tasked with conducting SIGINT is the National Security Agency, which is an entity within the Department of Defense. This agency was created in 1952 by a memorandum issued by President Truman. The impetus was the realization that the military and the CIA were wasting US resources by jointly targeting the same adversaries by SIGINT. So the very intelligent decision was reached that SIGINT should be conducted by only one organization and so a joint civilian/military agency was created.

Because the memo creating the NSA was itself a classified document, the very existence of the NSA was a secret for many years. This gave rise to the joke that NSA stood for "No Such Agency."

What are the most important issues in SIGINT?

Unlike HUMINT, in which we receive information we know the source wanted us to have, information obtained by SIGINT is assumed to be something the source did not think we were "listening in on."

As such, it has an automatic degree of reliability, provided we are interpreting it correctly. And therein lies the real challenge with SIGINT.

Imagine the last email you sent to a very close friend. You referred to things you and your friend know well. Maybe you made inside jokes, based on anecdotes going all the way back to high school!

Now imagine some Russian SIGINT agent somewhere managed to intercept that email. (And

I hope the Russians don't have that capability!) First off, if she doesn't know English very well, she can't make any sense of the email at all! But they can probably hire competent linguists.

Even if you used well-known English words, you may have been using them to refer to things which, not knowing the background context, would make no sense to another person. In other words, you can say something to a friend, knowing that the friend will successfully "read between the lines," but that Russian SIGINT agent will report that she knows all the words and simply doesn't understand what the letter is really saying.

And if you used very vernacular slang in your email, she may run into trouble for other reasons. This Russian agent could have learned English starting in middle school. She might have majored in English in college. She may speak it excellently, with just the tiniest hint of an accent.

But she still can't completely understand your email. Why? Because there are things that only a full native speaker, growing up in the country in question, will be able to hear or read and understand.

How do I know she doesn't understand your email? Because I, with a PhD and years of Arabic study, regularly faced things at the NSA that I could not understand. Don't get me wrong. I spent my entire day translating things well. I was promoted to GS-13 because of my skills. But there were regularly things I could not interpret because I am not a native speaker of Arabic. But luckily, that did not mean that crucial intelligence at the NSA could not be processed.

Let me assure you, dear reader, that working at the NSA are patriotic Americans of virtually every original nationality. I worked with women and men from every country of the Middle East. They became US Citizens and they offer their linguistic skills to the defense of our nation. And we should be grateful to them for their service. I am particularly grateful to them because, on many occasions, as a non-native speaker of Arabic, I needed their expertise to solve particularly difficult puzzles for our national security.

Lessons Learned

When you see or hear a communication sent from one person to another, there are numerous interpretive issues you need to consider. You may overhear an exchange that will only make sense if you are fully immersed in the culture of those involved. You may also hear only one side of a conversation. You could assume what the other side is saying and be completely wrong or completely right. Imagine the following brief exchange you could overhear. If all you heard was the B side, you would have to engage in speculation as to what the B side was responding to:

[A) When is the attack?]
B) At 9AM.
[A) Is the bomb ready?]
B) It is.

[A) When is the Wedding?]
B) At 9AM.
[A) Is it an open bar at the reception?]
B) It is.

Now, add in the possibility that the term "Wedding" could be a known cover term for "Attack" and "Open Bar" could mean "weapons ready" and you can begin to understand just how hard it is to interpret intelligence from within SIGINT.

In general, the implication of SIGINT is that great care must be taken when interpreting any information you receive. That is the same whether you are one of the intended recipients of the communication or whether you simply overhear a communication somehow. We must never forget the real possibility of a misunderstanding in either case.

An immediate application of SIGINT analysis to our personal and professional lives comes in the area of email correspondence. You've probably experienced the phenomenon of a spat that somehow resulted through an internet exchange. People who never had an angry word in person suddenly feel insulted by the tone they perceived online.

In all correspondence, it is helpful to take a step back and analyze the message as if you were not one of the parties involved. People can inadvertently come off as terse or insulting merely because they felt rushed to reply. We sometimes interpret our personal correspondence through the lens of our wider relationships and in the context of the previous communication that led to the most recent message. As a result, we may sometimes find fault where certainly none was intended.

In the final analysis, just like SIGINT agents, we receive forms of communication all the time which require a particular type of interpretation not ordinarily used in face-to-face interactions. We need to acknowledge the potential for misunderstandings connected to both the medium itself, as well as cultural and linguistic nuances.

It may sometimes be possible to deduce true information of value to our personal and professional lives by "reading between the lines" of the information we receive. But, more often, we need to exercise extreme caution when potentially overanalyzing our communications with others.

Applications for your Organization

SIGINT as nation states conduct it is not likely going to be a significant danger to your secrets from competitors directly. Depending, however, on the scale of your organization, nation states may, somewhere within the range of their overall priorities, target you on behalf of your competitors.

The response to this potential breach in security is to use cell phones with the highest possible level of encryption available. Reportedly, Angela Merkel inappropriately continued using an unencrypted phone, which was more susceptible to interception.[6] To be completely safe, one should communicate on electronic devices under the assumption that your worst enemy is listening. Your most valuable secret really can wait until you are face-to-face with an approved recipient of that information within a secure space.

---

[6] Source: https://www.thelocal.de/20131025/52577

CHAPTER SEVEN: OPERATIONS SECURITY (OPSEC)

Definition of OPSEC

Operations Security (OPSEC) concerns the observable aspects of an intelligence or military operation that, while not strictly classified themselves, can be used to deduce something classified or can be exploited by an adversary in some way.

The classic and frequently cited example of an OPSEC failure is how it was possible to deduce that the 1st Gulf War in 1991 was about to commence.

Frank Meeks, owner of several Domino's franchises in the DC area, told the *Chicago*

Tribune on January 16, 1991 that he believed the start of the war was imminent based solely on the uptick of pizza sales delivered to government offices.[7] The war started the very next day.

Each time I went on overseas deployments, I was sent to CIA Headquarters to take what was called the "Overseas Safety Course." I will not divulge many details of what I learned there because I would not want our adversaries to know what we study in an attempt to conduct appropriate Operations Security while abroad. In short, I was told how to conduct myself while abroad to minimize danger.

For instance, if you leave your house at exactly the same time every day, you are making it easier for an adversary to target you. Many of our intelligence agents overseas are in countries that are virtual police states. As such, our enemies there cannot just hang out for hours on end waiting for the chance to strike. Authorities will become suspicious and will investigate. But if a US

---

[7] "Crusty D.C Veteran Says War is Near." *Chicago Tribune*, January 16, 1991. http://articles.chicagotribune.com/1991-01-16/news/9101050225_1_frank-meeks-pizza-pentagon

person leaves their house at exactly 7:20AM every day, it lets our adversaries plan to arrive just a minute before, conduct an attack, and then flee. And so, good OPSEC implies that you should change your departure time regularly so that anyone planning an action will be quite hesitant to target you.

Lessons Learned

We all have secrets, personal and professional, that we do not want the entire world to know about. The lesson of OPSEC is that our secrets can sometimes be deduced by those around us if we do not exercise considerable care with seemingly irrelevant details.

We may think we are keeping our personal and professional matters confidential merely by carefully divulging them only to highly trusted friends and colleagues. But what seemingly innocent behaviors, if observed and interpreted together, might be telegraphing our secrets to others?

As a teacher, for instance, if I give a test only on Tuesdays, announced or not, the students will start to take notice and plan accordingly. I have students who strategically plan sick days around avoiding various assessments.

OPSEC indicators are essentially what professional poker players refer to as a "Tell." A "Tell" is any observable change in another player's appearance, demeanor, or conduct that the person subconsciously displays in conjunction with having good or bad cards in their hand. Knowing other players' "Tells" can be a valuable tool when betting against them.

Even outside the highly stressful field of high stakes professional poker, all of us have subconscious "Tells" that may be advertising our internal attitudes in the home and workplace. We may perhaps want our spouse or best friend to know how we are feeling, but not necessarily our boss. Practicing good OPSEC on the job would mean we need to inventory our own "Tells" and control them. (Taken to the next level, one could also theoretically use a knowledge of their own "Tells" to mislead someone intentionally, as in the example of the Double Cross System described in chapter 5.)

Top Secrets

Keeping our lives confidential has only become more problematic in the modern age. My advice to anyone truly wanting to conduct good personal OPSEC is that, for starters, you should use only the strictest possible privacy settings available in your social media profiles. And then you should still, as I do, never include any information there which you do not want the entire world to know.

We are also constantly showing the world clues about our personal lives with every site we visit on the internet and even those things that we order online. The department store Target reportedly built an algorithm that could predict, based on seemingly unconnected online purchases, whether a customer was pregnant.

Reportedly, an angry father went to a local Target to complain that his daughter had received a mailed advertisement implying she was pregnant. The manager apologized on behalf of Target and when he called the man again a few days later to reiterate the apology, learned from the man that it turned out she was pregnant after all.[8]

Applications for your Organization

You should already have instructed your employees to minimize discussion of sensitive work related matters on social media. But the lesson of OPSEC is that secrets can also be deduced from seemingly innocent information. If you are high level enough, aspects of your regular schedule could send a signal that something big is happening in your organization. If you post a picture of your restaurant plate while out with your husband every single Tuesday, but then don't do so one week because you stayed at work late to finalize that big product launch, you may have just telegraphed that fact to a shrewd competitor who happens to be monitoring that feed.

An important response to that potential breach is to make sure you are always using the strictest

---

[8] "How Companies Learn Your Secrets," by Charles Duhigg. *The New York Times Magazine*, February 16. 2012.
http://www.nytimes.com/2012/02/19/magazine/shopping-habits.html

security settings within each social media platform. Also, double check that everyone you are friends with there is really someone you know and trust.

So, in the final analysis, practicing perfect OPSEC will end up becoming increasingly difficult in the computer age. But OPSEC is certainly an area where doing *something* is always better than doing *nothing*. Even just minimizing clues about our attitudes and plans can help us preserve our advantage in a workspace setting. Being on the lookout for lapses in OPSEC by others might also help us get ahead.

CHAPTER EIGHT: DECIPHERING SECRET CODES

I've always been fascinated by mysteries. And even before I went to the NSA, I had published my proposed solution to an ancient linguistic puzzle. The holy book of Islam, the Qur'an, contains a series of seemingly random letters that begin several of the chapters. I published an article in 1996 in which I argued that the letters were not really random at all, but were ordered lists of the abbreviated names of people consulted as sources for the wording of these chapters.[9]

---

[9] "A New Investigation into the 'Mystery Letters' of the Qur'an," by Keith Massey, in *Arabica, Vol. 43 No. 3.* (1996), pp. 497–501.

I would later find out that the very fact that I had official academic publications contributed to the decision to include me in the new hires development program I described in chapters 1 and 2.

But when I came to the NSA, I had the opportunity to take a week-long course in cryptographic methods. It taught me all the techniques of how to both encrypt and decrypt a message that had been used up to the period of World War II, when early computers took over the task. And I learned how to spot and exploit patterns that could unlock the key to a secret message.

Cracking a "Secret" Code on the Job!

While still at the NSA, I had the opportunity to put my new talents to the test. In a December while I was there, a message had been sent to some government agency. It was a seemingly random series of numbers, apparently a code of some kind. The NSA sent it out to all employees with a request that people try to decipher it. I looked at it and immediately spotted that several of the "words" started with the same two numbers.

I followed the hypothesis that this was a message in the Arabic language. The word in Arabic for "the" is *al-*. And it's prefixed to the word it modifies. So I wrote out AL everywhere I saw that pattern, including other places those numbers appeared. I spotted that there was a word in the message that was only three letters long, but it started with "AL." I assumed this was the common Arabic preposition "to" (transliterated as ALI). From there other words opened up. Within minutes I had deciphered the message. It stated that nuclear bombs would be going off in Washington, New York, and Chicago.

My heart was racing as I rushed to the office that had sent out this cryptographic challenge. As I was approaching the door, a woman I had worked with previously was also arriving there. I knew her to be a skilled cryptographer. I blurted out half the message. She shouted out the rest. We burst through the door and presented our findings jointly to the requesting office.

We would later learn that the "code" in question was a known "aspirational message," meaning, it was something that Jihadists had been posting widely on open sources, with high hopes but no credibility (obviously, since it didn't happen). The particular form that we had "deciphered" had defaulted the Arabic letters to numbers during a copy and paste function. In other words, this message had been accidentally, and unintentionally, turned into a cryptographic puzzle.

Even so, the office that issued the challenge was grateful that analysts at the NSA had been able to decipher the puzzle and at least relieve the Intelligence Community that we had not missed some important secret message. The other analyst and I were jointly given a cash reward for our efforts that made Christmas that year a lot more merry.

Other Decipherments

Since I have left the NSA, I have published proposed decipherments of a number of ancient mysteries. For instance, I published a proposed decipherment of the enigmatic Ezerovo Ring, one of the few examples of Dacian writing.[10] And I even released a mathematical interpretation of the oldest example of human writing ever discovered, the Tartaria Tablets.[11]

My most recent effort, and by far the most notable, is my proposed decipherment of the 250 year old mystery known as the Shugborough Inscription. My solution to this enigma was reported in the *Birmingham Post* and I was interviewed by the BBC's *World Update* concerning my research.[12]

---

[10] "Further Evidence for an 'Italic' Substratum in Romanian," by Keith Massey in *Philologie im Netz* 43/2008, pp. 11-16.
http://web.fu-berlin.de/phin/phin43/p43t2.htm

[11] To study my proposals, visit my website:
http://www.keithmassey.com/decipherments.html/

[12] "200-Year-Old Mystery of Shugborough Code 'Solved'," by Mike Lockley. *Birmingham Post*, December 21, 2014.
http://www.birminghampost.co.uk/news/regional-affairs/200-year-old-mystery-shugborough-code-solved-8319385/
BBC World Update interview with Dan Damon on 12/24/2014.

Applying Cryptography To Your Situation

You can use the principles of decipherment to achieve personal success in your own context. You see, decipherment is the process of bringing into the open something that is hidden. Yes, it may ordinarily describe bringing a secret message into plain view, but we all have secrets to success in our lives that we wish we could crack. And the methods of decipherment have broader applications to assist us.

The Cryptographic Method

So let's study what we code-breakers do when we approach an unsolved mystery. I'm going to use my research on the Shugborough Inscription as a test case to describe the steps of decipherment and how they can be applied to whatever you want to solve for your own person or professional needs.

Background on the Shugborough Inscription

In the 1700's, a British adventurer Thomas Anson commissioned the building of a monument on his property at Shugborough Castle. The monument itself was a marble relief based on a painting, *The Arcadian Shepherds*, by Nicholas Poussin.

But carved into a marble slab below the relief was a series of enigmatic letters. The likes of Charles Darwin and Charles Dickens have attempted to make sense of them. In more recent times, former Bletchley Park code breakers Oliver and Sheila Lawn studied them and also did not arrive at a conclusion.[13]

Here are the letters in question:

O.U.O.O.S.V.A.V.V.

Slightly below these letters, and offset at the ends are two more letters:

D M

---

[13] "Cryptic Code Stumps Experts," by Bootie Cosgrove-Mather. *CBS News*, May 14, 2004. http://www.cbsnews.com/news/cryptic-code-stumps-experts/

Step One: Determining Possible Source Language

In order to decipher anything, you will eventually have to take a gamble on what language you think the puzzle is made up of. As in the case of the Arabic cryptogram I described above, I only succeeded because my guess was correct. If the message had been French, my method could never have succeeded. Now, we can sometimes guess on the language that might be behind the puzzle based on letter counts and frequencies. For instance, if you find in an enciphered message that there are 26 different characters that appear, there is a reasonably good chance that it is a language that uses the Latin alphabet. If you find that your message contains considerably more than 26, it might be something like Arabic, which contains consonants that don't exist at all in English and has letters in its alphabet to represent them.

Now, as a trained code-breaker at the NSA, but also as a scholar of the Latin language, I looked at this data and searched for patterns both cultural and epigraphical.

I immediately concluded that the D and M were a known commodity. Funeral inscriptions from ancient Rome abound with these two letters. They stand for:

D: Dis
M: Manibus

Dis Manibus is a Latin phrase meaning "For the Ancestral Spirits." The Manes were understood as one's own ancestral spirits to whom you should make prayers and sacrifices for protection and prosperity.

But this was a clue for the whole inscription. D M is Latin. And that convinced me that the cryptic series of letters were encoding a Latin sentence as well.

Lessons Learned

You've just heard me conclude that a cryptic series of letters are probably Latin because of my near certainty that two prominent letters near the inscription are very likely Latin themselves.

How can you apply this step to your situation? As you go through life, you frequently have to make decisions and execute moves based on scanty data. But guess what? If you don't make those moves, you've still made a move. Inaction is itself an action.

There is a quote from Shakespeare's *Julius Caesar* that inspires me on this point:

> There is a tide in the affairs of men.
> Which, taken at the flood, leads on to fortune;
> Omitted, all the voyage of their life
> Is bound in shallows and in miseries.
> On such a full sea are we now afloat,
> And we must take the current when it serves,
> Or lose our ventures.[14]

Whatever riddle you need to solve for your own personal or professional success will not wait for you. You must eventually act or accept the consequences of inaction. And you should act from

---

[14] William Shakespeare, *Julius Caesar* Act 4, Scene 3.

the most likely solution, even if you do not have enough evidence yet for full certainty.

And so, are there other ways to interpret the D and the M? Yes. But they're weak and contrived. The D and the M stand for **Dis Manibus**.

Does that necessarily mean the whole inscription is Latin?

No. But to assume the inscription is *not* Latin and then expend significant energy based on that assumption would be quite poor methodology in this particular case.

Again, you are forced to make these snap decisions every day of your life. And the most reliable methodology is to interpret the data based on what we call Ockham's Razor.[15] In short, the simplest and most obvious solution is probably the true solution, unless you have compelling evidence otherwise.

---

[15] Named after the medieval philosopher William of Ockham (1287-1347).

I followed Ockham's Razor to the conclusion that the whole inscription is likely Latin. But from there, my breakthrough relied on knowledge gained through previous research.

Step Two: Find and Exploit Possible Patterns

It is possible to encrypt a message so well that patterns in the original message become virtually non-existent. This is precisely why the Allies only managed to finally read the Nazis' communications after Alan Turing back-engineered the computer that was encrypting the messages.[16]

But if the level of encryption is weak enough, not only may there be patterns, but the patterns themselves will be the key to decipherment.

And so I looked again at the Shugborough Inscription:

---

[16] A story wonderfully described and portrayed in the movie *The Imitation Game* (2014).

O.U.O.S.V.A.V.V.

I asked myself, have I seen anything like this before? And I let that sink in. I took an inventory of exactly what we have in this inscription. Here are the letters we are looking at, in order of occurrence and frequency:

O: 2
U: 1
S: 1
V:3
A: 1

The code-breaker in me zeros in on that "V: 3." The most commonly occurring letter could be an important clue.

Why do I assume that? Let me pose this point. If you are driving somewhere, and you see a single police car having pulled over another car, you assume that you are looking at a simple traffic stop.

But if you look ahead and you see three police cars, lights blaring, in front of and behind a car, chances are, you assume that something bigger than a speeding ticket is going on.

It's the same thing with decryption. It may indeed be a pure coincidence that there are 3 V's in the message. They may not be a clue which will help us decipher the piece. But to ignore them entirely because they *might* not be a clue would be, again, quite poor methodology. A code-breaker is going to first chase down the possible significance of a clear pattern. If nothing comes of it, then you are back to square one.

I next zero in on the first two letters. What's exciting to me as a Latin scholar is that the inscription has both the letter U and the letter V. You see, very ancient Latin inscriptions would have made no distinction at all between those letters. The fact that the Shugborough Inscription does contain both U and V is a massive gift to us as code-breakers. That's because Latin words that start with V are *always* followed by a vowel. And Latin words that begin with U are *always* followed immediately by a consonant.

As an NSA code-breaker and scholar of the Latin language, I'm thinking, we're half way home!

Step Three:
Make and Test Proposals

This is the point in the process in which one must finally take the available information and craft possible solutions with the data and see if anything compelling emerges.

When I describe Step Four as "Make and Test Proposals," I mean to say that frequently one may arrive at a possible interpretation or solution of a code, but the product fails to convince many others that the decipherment really was correct. And if that happens, it does not mean that the decipherment is invalid. It may also mean that the decipherment, while technically possible, is not valid and the code breaker should explore other possibilities.

As I started to surmise possible words behind the code, I realized that I had a secondary clue to the meaning of the first two letters of this inscription. I had recently been researching Latin inscriptions for a book I wrote on ancient prayer practices.[17] And during my research, I had seen an inscription that began with the same two letters as the one at Shugborough:[18]

Shugborough Inscription
O.U.O.S.V.A.V.V.
Ancient North African Latin Inscription
O.V.B.Q[19]

The ancient North African inscription was an abbreviation for:

Oro Ut Bene Quiescat.
I pray that she may rest well.

As I looked at the rest of the letters, I asked myself, "Where are there three V's prominently in Latin literature?"

---

[17] *Praying Our Fathers: The Secret Mercies of Ancestral Prayer,* by Keith Massey (Lingua Sacra Publishing: 2014).

[18] Remember, in ancient times, both U and V were written with a V.

[19] *Roman Africa*, by Alexander Graham (London: 1902), p. 152.

I immediately thought of the famous quote from Julius Caesar:

Veni, Vidi, Vici![20]
I came, I saw, I conquered!

But that phrase did not seem to match the prayer context of the opening that I was pretty confident in. I needed something of a religious nature. And then I remembered the Latin rendering of John 14:6, "I am the Way, the Truth, and the Life":

Ego sum Via et Veritas et Vita.

So I decided to populate the rest of the letters with basic Latin that would somehow use the words of that famous quote and also produce a grammatical sentence.

Here's what I proposed:

Oro Ut Omnes Sequantur Viam Ad Veram Vitam.
I pray that all may follow the Way to True Life.

---

[20] Suetonius, *Divus Julius* 37.

Conclusion to the Shugborough Inscription

I believe my proposal provides a sensible and credible interpretation of this long-standing mystery. My interpretation produces a straightforward and grammatical sentence, all parts of which are attested in tomb inscriptions and texts predating or contemporary with the creation of the Shugborough Inscription. [21]

Lessons Learned

Let's review the key elements I used to arrive at my proposal to see how they might help you decipher the secret to your own personal and professional success.

Knowledge

Knowing that the most ancient Latin inscriptions wrote a U as a V and also knowing that there was an ancient inscription that began

---

[21] To see the additional text sources, visit my website: http://www.keithmassey.com/decipherments.html

O.V was the very key to unlocking the secrets of the Shugborough Inscription.

And so, much of my success was based on knowledge I had gained accidentally through other projects. But what that means for all of us is that no learning is accidental! You simply never know when knowledge of an important fact will be the key to unlocking some considerable success. So if we want to succeed, regardless of our field, we need to read widely so that we can cross-fertilize what we know to achieve a new perspective on the areas we seek to master.

Patterns

The key to deciphering the Shugborough Inscription was the fact that the V occurred three times while no other letter was so common. Finding a passage in ancient literature with three V's was the key to finalizing my decipherment. But first spotting the pattern was the key component.

In our lives, we are surrounded by data. And we sometimes become so overwhelmed by the sheer volume of it that we fail to step back and try to spot the patterns that might guide us toward success.

Look for patterns in the data of your life. Repetitions of letters are the keys code-breakers study. What repetitions can help us decipher the secret to success in our lives?

As an example of repetition, is there a particular skill that you realize in retrospect you were recognized for several times in your life? It might just be that you are particularly good at that! And maybe you need to focus more energy there.

Spotting patterns around us is also a good way to boost our overall efficiency. For instance, if there are three copy machines at your work and the middle one always jams double-sided copies, spotting and knowing that pattern lets you select the most time-efficient machine for your job. (That might seem a trivial example, but I've seen numerous cases in my life of people who apparently have not spotted patterns such as that.)

Perhaps the most important take away from the concept of decipherment is simply to acknowledge that, for every problem, every challenge we may face, there is likely some solution out there. And if we do not at least try to solve it, someone else may beat us to it.

We rarely lose more by trying and failing. But we do lose by not trying. And to overcome a challenge, we will have to make decisions, make assumptions, and test hypotheses. And if we are wrong, and we do not find the solution, we are no worse off than when we started. And that should inspire us to persistence.

Chapter Nine: Living Your Cover

Definition of "Cover"

A "cover" in espionage refers to the *persona* that an undercover agent is overtly seeming to be while they covertly conduct espionage.

As I described above, the website of the Central Intelligence Agency openly describes the fact that members of the National Clandestine Service collect human intelligence overseas. The word "Clandestine" itself implies that the person is undercover, though the CIA site does not describe what these covers are (for obvious security reasons).

As a former member of the Intelligence Community, I know a lot about "cover" that I cannot write about. All I will say is that a search on the topic of "cover" in open source information, compared with Hollywood assumptions such as appear in spy movies, is a mixed bag of fact and pure fiction.

Who Conducts Undercover Operations?

The CIA openly admits they conduct clandestine operations overseas. Now, there are many other agencies of the US Government besides the CIA that do conduct *overseas* operations. For instance, my unclassified resume from the NSA, approved by the Office of Security there for public use, includes the line:

Served at an overseas field site.

But not every overseas operation would necessarily require that its employees be "undercover" the way a Clandestine Officer would be. For instance, many employees of the State Department are serving overseas. But they're not undercover.

How does "Cover" apply to my life?

A "cover" is a public *persona*. In the world of espionage, it is designed to conceal those who see the person from knowing that, in fact, this person is conducting espionage. But a "cover" is not necessarily, in and of itself, a complete lie.

An example from reported news explains my point. Valerie Plame openly describes herself as a former undercover officer of the CIA.[22]

According to media reports[23] and her own book, Ms. Plame was a functioning CIA agent

---

[22] *Fair Game: How a Top CIA Agent Was Betrayed By Her Own Government,* by Valerie Plame (New York: 2008).

She submitted her book for pre-publication approval to the CIA, though a caveat at the beginning of the book states that "Nothing in the contents should be construed as asserting or implying US Government authentification of information or Agency endorsement of the author's views." I have a similar disclaimer at the beginning of this book.

[23] "Subject of C.I.A. Leak Testifies on Capitol Hill," by David Stout. *The New York Times*, March 16, 2007. http://www.nytimes.com/2007/03/16/washington/16 cnd-plame.html?_r=0

while simultaneously presenting herself as the wife of a US diplomat, the mother of twins, and an expert in non-conventional weapons.

But here's my point. She was all those things! The fact that she was additionally a CIA agent does not negate the reality of her "cover."

Lessons Learned

All of us go through our lives under varying modes of "cover." For example, I'm going to admit something to you that I'm not proud of. I sometimes swear. I might as well be more honest. I swear all the time.

I'm a Latin teacher in a public high school. I'm going on my tenth year. And never, not once, have I dropped the F-Bomb in a class. You could say, when I teach, I am undercover as someone who *doesn't* swear. But my *persona* as a teacher is not fraudulent because I exercise discipline and remain professional there. I am known in my school as someone who daily greets people by name with a smile. And that is indeed who I am, even if I let off steam later and grumble a bit about my students from time to time.

And so, we all wear various "covers" in our lives. We are compartmentalized and that's okay. But perhaps a valuable life lesson from the world of espionage is that we will be most successful when our "cover" is as authentic as possible. Valerie Plame was undercover, but her cover did not involve a different name.

The practical reason for avoiding cover names is that you've spent your entire life answering to something and under pressure we would all have a tendency to screw it up! So, if I ever happened to have been under some type of cover, and someone had shouted out "Keith!" in an airport, I would have instinctively turned around to see who called me. And if my "cover" involved me holding a passport with the name "Andrew Valquist" on it, I might have blown that cover. But that never happened because I have never gone anywhere, even on official NSA business, with any name besides my own on my passport.

For example, I once visited our counterparts at the British equivalent of the NSA, known as GCHQ. I flew to the UK not with my blue tourist passport, but with an "Official" passport, which had a reddish brown cover. And the name "Keith Massey" was inside it.

Another piece of what it means to "live your cover" is the realization that you really can choose the *persona* that you present to the world. And you can enrich and augment that *persona* to become the person you truly want to be.

One day, years ago, while I was still working on my doctoral dissertation, I went to the post office and a man there was trying to find out how to send money to his mother in Mexico. He spoke very limited English and the employee there at the post office was actually going out of his way to make the process difficult for the man. I wanted to be able to assist this person, but I could not. Because I did not speak any Spanish at the time.

I was struck by a disconnect within my *persona*. Here I was, by any objective definition of the term, "highly educated." And yet I spoke no Spanish. I left there that day resolved that I needed to change that fact. I got some books and I worked. I crammed. I memorized vocabulary. I recited verb paradigms. I worked at least two hours a day on this project. And I arrived within a year at a highly functional speaking ability in Spanish.

My *persona*, my "cover," had not previously involved me speaking Spanish. Now it does. My "cover" remains a work in progress, toward becoming the person I want to be.

Chapter Ten: Resources for Learning More

I have provided an overview of some of the sub-disciplines of espionage. If you would like to delve in much more deeply on further facets of the topic, as well as fully verse yourself on matters of internet and computer security, explore the following websites.

Espionage

Human Intelligence (HUMINT)

The website of the Central Intelligence Agency (CIA) is a treasure trove of (unclassified) information on the history and operations of this

organization. Visit the site at:
https://www.cia.gov/
Particularly valuable on the CIA site is their World Factbook. Begin exploring it here:
https://www.cia.gov/library/publications/resources/the-world-factbook/

Intelligence Explained

The Secret Intelligence Service (SIS), often referred to as MI6, is the British equivalent of the CIA. Their website includes a terrific interactive page showing how their agency operates with other partners in a typical case study. Experience it here:
https://www.sis.gov.uk/intelligence-explained.html#section-02

Signals Intelligence (SIGINT)

The National Security Agency (NSA) describes their mission in an unclassified fashion, but also features an impressive educational outreach. Visit the site at: https://www.nsa.gov/

How Does an Analyst Catch a Terrorist?

The British equivalent of the NSA is known as the Government Communication Headquarters (GCHQ). They work very closely with their NSA counterparts (for example, for a period of time at the NSA my boss was a GCHQ agent!).The Brits have their own rules regarding classification issues and there is an excellent feature on the GCHQ website that describes in detail how a SIGINT analyst catches a terrorist, something you won't find, for instance, on the NSA website. Read this fascinating account of "How Does an Analyst Catch a Terrorist: https://www.gchq.gov.uk/features/how-does-analyst-catch-terrorist

Imagery Intelligence (IMINT)

I didn't discuss IMINT in this book, but the National Reconnaissance Office (NRO) operates .systems of spy satellites providing SIGINT to the NSA but also images to the National Geospatial-Intelligence Agency (NGA) Explore the websites of these organizations to learn more: https://www.nro.gov/ and https://www.nga.mil/

Keith Massey

Computer and Internet Security

Email System Security

The National Institute of Standards and Technology (NIST) has published a comprehensive set of recommendations to be followed to optimize email security by system managers. The document includes helpful appendices featuring a glossary of terminology, an email security checklist, and commonly used acronym. Study these recommendations at:
http://csrc.nist.gov/publications/nistpubs/800-45-version2/SP800-45v2.pdf

Business E-Mail Compromise (BEC)

The Federal Bureau of Investigation (FBI) provides this eye-opening account of how businesses are targeted for fraud through spoofed emails. The page includes helpful protocols to avoid falling victim to such a scam:
https://www.fbi.gov/news/stories/business-e-mail-compromise

The Long History of the "Nigerian General" Scam

When I was awaiting the background check for my security clearance, I received, for the first but not last time in my life, the classic "Nigerian General" Advance Scam in my email. It freaked me out so much that I called the FBI local office to report it, just to make sure it wasn't part of an NSA test of my integrity. They assured me it was something to just ignore. But many people are not aware that versions of this scam are at least 200 years old; the internet has just aided in its proliferation. Here's the background:
https://www.bostonglobe.com/ideas/2013/05/18/the-long-weird-history-nigerian-mail-scam/C8bIhwQSVoygYtrlxsJTlJ/story.html

OnGuardOnline

The Federal Trade Commission (FTC) provides a terrific collection of tips on overall computer and internet security, entitled OnGuardOnline. Visit it here:
https://www.consumer.ftc.gov/features/feature-0038-onguardonline

Identity Theft

If you are the victim of Identity Theft, Knowledge is Power. According to Regular E, Section 205.6 of the Federal Reserve, in the event of fraudulent withdrawal of funds from your accounts, you are liable for only $50.00 of loss, provided you report this to your financial institution in a timely fashion. Check your credit rating regularly and report anything suspicious the moment you see it. If you do suspect a problem, follow the advice outlined on this website, sponsored by the FTC: https://www.identitytheft.gov/

Be CERTain about Security

Within the Department of Homeland Security (DHS) there is a fantastic and helpful organization known as the United States Computer Emergency Readiness Team (US-CERT), dedicated to providing the public with the very latest information and products to protect against cyber threats. Visit their site here : https://www.us-cert.gov/

Appendix: The Three Month Productivity Plan of the Ancients

In chapter 2 of this book, I described the three months I spent in Iraq. They were days of toil, stress, and fear. But they were also days in which I accomplished an extraordinary amount of work.

In this appendix I will describe how my experience in Iraq led me to discover that ancient peoples knew and practiced three month campaigns to maximize productivity. And you can apply this to your own personal and professional life as well.

I've placed this information in an appendix because it is, strictly speaking, not directly connected to the world of espionage. I first encountered this plan while serving at the NSA. And I confirmed the historical significance of this plan using research skills I honed while working as an intelligence officer for the government. But the Three Month Productivity Plan of the Ancients is a bonus to what I've presented elsewhere in the book.

Introduction

While I was serving as an Intelligence Officer in Iraq:

I had worked 90 consecutive eleven hour days.

I had gotten into the best shape of my adult life and lost thirty pounds.

I had learned functional Romanian.

I had passed the final Arabic certification test—with honors.

And then I came home. It seemed suddenly strange at first, back at home and in my regular job, to work only eight hours a day. And it certainly seemed unusual to have so much free time at my disposal.

I continued my Romanian studies at home. After work and after going for a long power walk which was now supposed to substitute for the work out I did in Iraq, I would sit down and try to memorize new vocabulary cards.

Within days of coming home, however, I was noticing a disturbing trend. First of all, left to my own devices, I was eating as much as I wanted. I was not working out as much. And I certainly wasn't studying as much.

Now, apart from the 90 consecutive eleven hour days, everything else I had accomplished was all on my own time. And it had happened on less disposable free time than I had now. But by the end of my first month back home, it was evident to me that I was not nearly as productive as I had been back in Iraq.

But that wasn't really the end of the world. I was doing well in my new office of Counter-Terrorism back at the NSA. I worked eight hour days, Monday through Friday. (Sometimes I took a weekend shift, and that was how I happened to be working on the Saturday I describe in chapter 3.)

After work I was spending my free time in a combination of recreative and learning activities. And if I was not learning Romanian at the same pace as I had achieved in Iraq, it was still not the end of the world.

But what puzzled me is why I was able to do so much more there in Iraq on so much less time.

Some of the reasons were obvious. Even if I was working only eight hour days now, back in Iraq I walked from my bed to my work desk in literally thirty seconds. Back in Iraq, I just sat down to eat at regular intervals, without ever having to prepare a meal for myself. Now, back home, I was spending ten minutes each way driving to work and cooking my own supper at the end of the day.

But that couldn't begin to explain the dramatic drop off in productivity I was seeing.

And then I realized something. The question wasn't why I was doing so little *here*. I was a highly performing professional at the United States' communications intelligence Spy Agency. I had nothing to be ashamed of.

The question was, why had I been able to do such an extraordinary amount of personal enrichment *there*, on top of a grueling work schedule that seemed to leave little time for anything besides work and sleep?

The issue haunted me, but I settled into my life.

On December 18th, 2004, my wife Adriana and I were married civilly, my twin brother Kevin officiating at a ceremony attended by my entire family in Madison, Wisconsin.

On January 2nd, 2005, we were married religiously in a ceremony at a monastery in Bucharest, Romania.

I explained in chapter 3 the financial reasons why it made sense to both of us to continue in our lives as they were, me living in Maryland and her in New Jersey. For the time being we would see each other on weekends while we mutually decided what we would eventually change so that we would be together full time.

In 2006, I left the NSA after four years of service there to take a job as a Latin teacher in New Jersey. The salary, calculating in the benefits and pension, made the move financially virtually the same. Working at the NSA had been certainly the most interesting and exciting thing I had ever done in my life. But I was ready to move on into a quieter life.

And so I settled into a new career. I had more free time to pursue writing and research, which I enjoyed.

That's when I stumbled onto something puzzling. I was reading the *Natural History* of Pliny the Elder, a 1st century AD Roman writer. And there I learned that the Arcadians, one of the peoples of Ancient Greece, at one time used a three month block of time as their "year."[24] In other words, they ignored the obvious annual cycle of the seasons and planned their lives around three months instead.

I was still recalling the remarkable productivity I had experienced in Iraq. And to see that someone else had once viewed three months as an important interval of time was intriguing.

Ancient Lessons

Using several online search tools, I began an in-depth study of "three months" in ancient literature. To my amazement, three month references were everywhere. I started to catalogue and classify them, arriving at the following

---

[24] Pliny the Elder, *Natural History* 7.49.

common situations where three month intervals of time were recorded.

Armistices. In addition to the Arcadians planning all their time based on three months, it seemed that governments frequently used three month intervals for armistices with enemy states.[25]

Military Campaigns and Projects. In addition to civilian government, the militaries of ancient peoples frequently planned and acted based on an interval of three months.[26]

Military Pay. Three months was the normal unit of time for military payment schedules.[27]

---

[25] Xenophon, *Agesilaus* 1; Polybius, *Histories* 18.10; Livy, *The History of Rome* 30.38.

[26] Polybius, *Histories* 1.38 (three months to build a navy); Xenophon, *Hellenica* 1.1; Suetonius, *Divus Augustus* 10; Pliny the Elder, *Natural History* 7.2; Plutarch, *Theseus* 27; Josephus, *Antiquities of the Jews* 14.4.

[27] Xenophon, *Anabasis* 1.1, 1.2, 5.1, 15.18.

Provisions. Three months shows up as a frequent unit for issuing provisions of food to both civilians and military members.[28]

So I'd discovered that three months was an important unit of time for the ancients. But why? And what, if anything, did this say about my experience of productivity for three months in Iraq?

Three Months and Pyramid Power

Then I stumbled on the most startling example of all. According to Herodotus, an ancient Greek historian, the Egyptians had not built the Pyramids using slave labor, as is commonly assumed. Rather, the men who built the pyramids were hired workers who were fed diets of meat while on the project. They worked in gangs of a hundred thousand. And they were rotated in and out of the project ***at three month intervals***.[29]

---

[28] Aristotle, *Economics* 2; Caesar, *Gallic Wars* 1.5; Livy, *The History of Rome* 8.2, 9.43; Plutarch, *Crassus* 2.

[29] Herodotus, *The Histories* 2.124.

The organization of something as complicated and grueling as the building of the pyramids would have evolved over time in order to maximize efficiency and productivity.

At some point the discovery would have been made that keeping a team of workers on the project for four months caused productivity to plummet, injuries and accidents to multiply, and morale to sink. And they must also have discovered that workers really can go three months with the same level of production as when they did only two. This was especially true when the workers knew that they would end these efforts at three months.

And so, the people who completed what is still today one of the most extraordinary engineering feats of human history had discovered the magic number of efficiency and productivity. Whether this information was actually passed on or just rediscovered by military and civic planners in other times and places is not important.

It's a metaphysical law. One can achieve great things through a three month burst of energy.

Repeating the Experiment

I had learned that the collective wisdom of the ancient world confirmed my experience. I had been able to show extraordinary productivity under extreme pressure precisely because I knew that it was limited to just three months. Three months is still not exactly a short amount of time. But it's not a year. It's livable. It's doable. The people who built the pyramids knew it was a sort of magic number right at the cutting edge of human ability.

In addition to my full time job teaching Latin, I had begun teaching a night course in Arabic at the local community college. In late fall of 2007, the director of world languages there asked me if I would be willing to teach two courses the following semester. This would mean two nights a week from 6 to 9PM.

I was a bit hesitant because, as one of the Senior Class advisors at the high school that year, I knew that the Spring would include evening events I would be required to attend. I also knew that I would need that Spring to take an online course in Language Teaching Methodology to receive my Standard Certificate to teach Latin. It all seemed a bit much. But I assumed that, if necessary, my progress on the online course could be put off for weeks as needed. This would turn out to be false.

Then, in early January came exciting news. I was offered the opportunity to write the book *Intermediate Arabic for Dummies*. Never before had I written a book for a major publisher like Wiley Publishing, and I knew nothing about the schedule for how such a project is to be completed. But it was an opportunity I simply could not pass up.

As January turned into February, it was increasingly clear to me that I had seriously overextended myself. It turned out that the online course would require five to ten hours a week and included assignments due each week no later than midnight on Saturday. In other words, I couldn't postpone the course at all.

The contract I signed with Wiley Publishing required me to submit the chapters of the book in four batches (Quarter 1 [Q1], Q2, etc.) at the end of each month, starting in February. Add in the fact that I was teaching Arabic at the community college now every Tuesday and Thursday night and that I needed to attend at least one nightly event every month for the Senior Class. And there was still the matter of a full time job as a Latin teacher!

And it became immediately clear, as I began work on the book, that this project alone was going to demand no less than twenty hours a week of my time.

I stumbled through February and managed to meet my deadlines. But I was scared. There simply weren't enough hours in the day to do all that I had to do.

The Three Month Productivity Plan of the Ancients

And then I remembered the secret of the three month campaign. I had three months of hell to endure, March, April, and May. If I could get through it, everything I was doing would be done. The online course would conclude in the middle of May. The Arabic teaching also. I was supposed to deliver just a few random pieces like the dictionaries and my biography for the Dummies book by the end of June. But that would no longer be a crisis since I would be done with all the other things.

My problem was how to survive March, April, and May. And the solution was to repeat the experiment I had accidentally performed in Iraq.

It was March 1st. I must endure the pressures and demands of each day, each day completing work on all the projects. For the sake of health, I decided that I could not work past 11:00PM. That is when I must go to sleep. But I used to enjoy watching television and sipping a glass of red wine in the early evening when I was free. That was now a luxury that my three month campaign could not include.

My Weekly Schedule

Sunday

The schedule would have to be as follows. I could not stop going to Church on Sunday. I love it too much. As an Eastern Orthodox, our service is two hours long. So I would have to get up in the morning and do work for two hours before then spending two hours at church. I had no choice. And whereas I used to enjoy talking with parishioners over coffee for an hour afterwards, I no longer could do that. I would have to leave immediately after the Sunday service and go home to work the rest of the day until 11:00PM.

I honored the Sabbath day by not missing Church. But there was no way I could possibly complete all my tasks with even one full day off work for the next three months.

Monday

My weekly commute starts at 5:30 to beat New York-bound traffic. But I would have to get all school work done at school, to leave time at home only for the other projects. And then I would have to work until 11:00PM.

Tuesday

Tuesday after school I went straight to the community college. In the two hours before the Arabic class started, I could get work done on the online course. Then, I realized I needed to find a way to make that Arabic book and the courses I was teaching overlap somehow. I would beta test the exercises I was crafting for the book on my Arabic students and plan lessons around what I was writing for the book at that time. And when I got home from the community college, I still had at least an hour and a half of productive time left before sleep.

Wednesday, Thursday, Friday

Wednesday would be like Monday. Thursday would be like Tuesday. Friday would be like Monday because for the next three months I did not have the luxury of what I used to call a weekend.

Saturday

Saturday would be a day to do nothing but work. All day long. By the end of that day I would also have to finish that week's requirements in the online course.

But I needed to remind myself continuously, every day as I endured this schedule, that this was not the rest of my life. This was exactly three months, just like Iraq. And it's livable. It's doable.

What followed was three months of hell. But I lived through it. I did it.

I delivered Q2 at the end of March. I built a few fake sick days into my Latin job, using those days to work only on the book. In April there was a Spring Break that gave me an entire week to even get ahead a bit on my projects. I delivered Q3 at the end of April. May saw the end of the college courses and the online course, with the immediate result of two more nights for work on the book in the last two weeks of that month. I delivered Q4 at the end of May.

And it was June 1st. I still had my regular full time job, but in June everything is winding down. I had gotten an A in my online course. All I had left on the book was to construct dictionaries and submit a biography and the acknowledgements page. There would still be editing and revising deep into the summer. But the bulk of the work was done.

And I realized that the three month campaign had been the only thing that got me through that period of time. It really does work.

Apply the Three Month Productivity Plan of the Ancients to your own life

Three months of productivity in Iraq pointed me toward this secret formula. Research into ancient histories showed me that my experience was no accident. And repeating this experiment successfully confirmed to me the fact that we humans are capable of extraordinary bursts of productivity lasting three months, as long as we know there is light at the end of the tunnel.

So choose a collection of things you wish you could accomplish but somehow never find the time for. Commit yourself to regular work on those matters for a three month period. You can accomplish great things when you know this is not the rest of your life.

It's three months. It's livable. It's doable. Three months later, you will take a well-deserved break and marvel at your accomplishments.

www.ingramcontent.com/pod-product-compliance
Lightning Source LLC
Chambersburg PA
CBHW071500040426
42444CB00008B/1423